THE
BIRTH
FATHER'S
TALE

ANDREW WARD

Published by
British Association for Adoption & Fostering
(BAAF)
Saffron House
6-10 Kirby Street
London EC1N 8TS
www.baaf.org.uk

Charity registration 275689 (England and Wales) and SC039337 (Scotland)
© Andrew Ward, 2012

British Library Cataloguing in Publication Data
A catalogue record for this book is available from the British Library
ISBN 978 1 907585 41 8

Designed and typeset by Helen Joubert Design
Printed in Great Britain by TJ International

Trade distribution by Turnaround Publisher Services, Unit 3, Olympia
Trading Estate, Coburg Road, London N22 6TZ

BAAF is the leading UK-wide membership organisation for all those
concerned with adoption, fostering and child care issues.

Contents

Note about the author

Andrew Ward is a freelance writer. His many books include *Football Nation* (with John Williams), *Kicking and Screaming* (with Rogan Taylor) and *I'm on Me Mobile* (with Anton Rippon). He co-edited *The Day of the Hillsborough Disaster* (with Rogan Taylor and Tim Newburn) and has written five books for Portico's best-selling 'Strangest' series, including *Cricket's Strangest Matches* and *Golf's Strangest Rounds*. He is also a birth father.

A note on the text

Names and identifying characteristics have been changed in most cases. Louise Archer is an amalgam of key people who helped with the search.

Changes in legislation have meant that certain procedures depicted here may no longer be feasible. Advice on searching for birth relatives is available from the British Association for Adoption and Fostering (BAAF), NORCAP, registered adoption agencies or the Adoption and Fostering department of a local childrens' services department.

1

Spring 1997

I had high hopes of Louise Archer. She was a specialist in adoption matters and I'd been given glowing references for her. She had been described to me as a counsellor, philosopher, detective, friend and intermediary. What particularly appealed to me was that she worked outside the system. I wondered if all birth fathers felt like outsiders in the way I often did.

'As I said on the phone, I'm what they call a birth father,' I told Louise Archer, the first time we met. 'As a teenager I fathered a boy who was adopted. The first I heard of the pregnancy was shortly after he was born.'

'And you'd like to find your son?' said Louise.

'Yes, please. I'd like to meet him. I'd like to find out who he is. Is that something you can do?'

'I can try. I can do my best.'

'I'd like to do some of the groundwork myself,' I said. 'I'd like to be involved in the actual searching.'

'We can do it together.'

'I'd prefer the process to be as simple as possible,' I said. 'I'd like it to be just you and me and my birth son…and maybe the birth mother.'

'I understand. What's the mother's name?'

'Carol,' I said.

'Are you in touch with Carol?'

'Not since we divorced. I haven't seen her for twenty-five years.'

I let that one sink in.

'Did you see your son when he was a baby?' Louise asked.

'No.'

We were meeting in Louise Archer's house. From the outside it was a modest two-up, two-down terraced house with an attic. We were upstairs in what had originally been a small bedroom. The room had two chairs, a small blackboard on one wall and bookshelves. Half of me wanted to read all the books on adoption; the other half didn't think I had enough emotional strength.

'How much do you know about the adoption system?' Louise said.

'A little. But let's start from scratch.'

'OK. Your child was adopted in the late 1960s?'

'Yes.'

'Well, that was a peak period for adoptions in Britain,' Louise explained. 'In those days they were closed adoptions. The system has changed enormously since then. Adoptions are almost all open now and they tend to involve young children with difficulties rather than babies. In the 1960s the names of babies were changed and the tracks were swept over when they were adopted. It was like putting them in a police protection scheme.'

I nodded. I knew some of this already but I wanted to hear it all from Louise.

I said, 'Bad guys like me were punished and the good people took over the parenting.'

'That is how some people saw it.'

'That was how it felt.'

We had a quiet spell. I sensed that Louise was thoughtful and calm.

'I feel as though I've been in a mystery story for the past twenty-nine years,' I said. 'I've been the villain and the victim, forever searching for some sort of dénouement to my loss. Now I'd like to be the detective's sidekick.'

'I suppose I am a detective of sorts,' Louise said. 'I can find people and approach them on your behalf if that's what you want.

But I'm not going to do that until you're properly prepared and we've explored the pros and cons.'

'I think being a birth father has affected my whole adult being. I suspect it's shaped my relationships, my career decisions, my writing projects, my whole assembly of attitudes.'

'I'd like to look at those things along the way, while we search,' said Louise. 'First of all I would like you to think about why you want to do this. Take some quiet time to think about why you want to search.'

'I'll do that. Offhand, I think my life is stuck. I never seem to quite get it together. I need to deal with this part of my life. I just want to tell my birth son that he's been important to me, never far from my mind, that he's shaped my life, and that there has been an invisible hand over him, wishing him well. And I'm here if he wants contact. I often wonder if he's tried to search for me.'

'Very few adopted people search for their fathers first.'

'But maybe he's approached his birth mother or her parents.'

'He could track the birth mother's parents but I always encourage adopted people to find the birth mother directly first. Going via the birth mother's parents should be the last option.'

'I think the birth mother got married again soon after we divorced,' I said. 'I should be able to find out her new married name easily enough.'

'You can also search for divorces at Somerset House.'

'I wonder how the birth mother has handled it during all these years.'

'We would have to ask her,' Louise said. 'I expect she will remember him at birthdays and Christmas. It gets worse when they become eighteen and twenty-one. She may be stuck. She probably feels a great deal of loss. She may have no-one to talk to about it. Sometimes there is a trigger, a magazine article, whatever, that sparks off a memory and causes an emotional wall. Adoption causes people to lose their family and their roots.'

'I have a feeling that I should have done more at the time. It cost me my identity. I've never been a family man earning a wage and raising a family.'

It was like I was saying to myself that real men would have stood up to their responsibilities and kept the child. But deep down, I knew that I was given no real choice.

'Adoption is full of issues of self-worth and self-punishment,' Louise told me. 'Reunions trigger the loss too. Adoption is forever. You're never free of it; you just learn to cope in a different way. But a lot depends on the outcome of the search.'

'Do other birth fathers punish themselves?'

'There's very little written about birth fathers. There's more about birth mothers.'

'You said that a lot depends on the outcome of the search.'

'The adopted people who meet their birth parents often say that their birth parents felt right, smelt right and sounded right. It makes you think about genetics.'

'I keep wondering why I didn't do more at the time.'

'Why do you think that was?'

'I don't know. I was so young. Adoptive parents had most of the power and the money. Our parents were in charge.'

'Adulthood didn't legally start until twenty-one in those days.'

'I often fantasise about meeting him and how that might come about.'

'Before a reunion parents are often up and down emotionally, fantasising about how the child is, how the reunion might be. It's swimming around their head. They find it hard to concentrate on other things.'

'That sounds like me.'

We went quiet again.

'What is it that's brought you to me now?' Louise asked. 'Why are you wanting to search at this point in your life?'

'I think I've always been searching for him. Sometimes I stare at someone in the street and wonder if he's the one. I have been doing lots of surrogate searches.'

'But why now?'

I thought for a while. Here was a moment of truth. Do I cover up parts of my story, or do I go deeper?

'Something happened to me,' I said. 'I had a very strange experience about three years ago. I reacted very oddly and I think it was to do with the adoption.'

'Can you tell me about that?'

'I could try. I might find it easier to write it down. I'm a writer by trade. I do my crying on my own.'

'I'd be happy to read anything you want to write.'

'Wonderful. It's usually much harder for me to find a reader.'

I was already a convert to writing as therapy. As an adult I had always done pieces of personal writing and found them calming and cathartic. Two years earlier, while co-editing a book about a major disaster, I'd seen the value to victims of having their story told. The first stage of healing is having your narrative recognised and reified.

I also saw writing therapy as a cheap alternative to talk therapy. Writing could be done at any time (unlike face-to-face therapy) and it provided a tool for reflection years later. My file of personal writings was a chilling record that forced me to face up to the patterns in my life.

'Write me something about how that incident from three years ago changed you,' Louise said. 'And try to think about your reasons for searching. I'll ask you about those reasons the next time I see you.'

'I'll do my homework,' I said. 'I've never missed a deadline.'

'OK. Do that at your leisure.'

'What else can I do now?'

'Do you know where the adoption file on your son is held?'

'No.'

'Well, we could try to find out where it is. Where was he born?'

I told her.

She looked past my head to a wall map of Britain. I swivelled round and pointed to a spot on the map. Louise stood up and walked to her bookshelves. She took out a book by Georgina Stafford called *Where to Find Adoption Records* and we looked at where the files might be held.

'Many of the agencies of the 1960s closed when the number of adoptions dried up,' she said. 'Their files often reverted to nearby Social Services departments. Did you attend an interview at the adoption agency?'

'I did.'

'Where was that?'

We discussed my fuzzy memories of a meeting nearly thirty years ago. Afterwards Louise was confident she had identified the agency our adoption went through.

'Details of that interview should be in your son's file,' she told me. 'Do you know which court the adoption went through?'

'I know what the birth mother told me.'

I told Louise the court district.

'OK. Write to Social Services in the town where he was born, and write to Social Services in the town where the court order went through. I'll write the addresses down for you.' She copied from the book she was holding. 'Address your letters to the Adoption and Fostering Department,' she continued. 'Give them all the information they need – your full name, the birth mother's full name, your son's name at birth and his date of birth. Register your interest and ensure that your letter goes into the Social Services file. Some Social Services are sympathetic. The law says they must keep the file for seventy-five years.'

'I hope it won't take us that long,' I said.

But it had taken me twenty-nine of those years to reach this point. It was that long since my birth son had arrived in the world.

2

Irene

I met Irene when my birth son was twenty-three. She was a high-powered company director whose life was spent in fast lanes between the cultural capitals of the world. She had class, style and money. She drove a sports car, enjoyed art and theatre, and mixed in an Oxbridge dinner-party world of articulation warfare. She was athletic, hedonistic and unfathomable. She was also stunningly attractive.

'Ivan's asked me to go to Prague,' Irene told me one night, as we chatted over supper. It was a weekday evening so we were together in my writer's garret flat in Oxford. Irene returned to her London home for weekends but stayed with me during the week.

'Oh,' I said.

I was aware that Irene had spent time with Ivan while she was in London at weekends but I thought he was only a work contact of hers, one of her intellectual set, a man with problems who could be stimulating company. In London she probably gave other men the impression that she was independent and available.

'Are you going with him?' I asked.

'I don't know. I went to Prague a couple of years ago. I'd rather go somewhere else.'

'It's going to affect *our* relationship if you go,' I told Irene.

She continued to think aloud.

'He's got a fat belly,' she said. 'I don't think I want his stomach on top of me.'

Here was a girlfriend talking freely to me as if I was a counsellor or a father-figure. This happened a lot in my relationships. I listened, asked questions, appeared non-judgmental, and then a woman was sometimes shocked if I showed feelings. Otherwise I was like an unconditional parent.

'I'll plan a trip abroad for us,' I said, even though I had no money and we'd recently been to Cornwall. 'We'll go somewhere you haven't been.'

Irene had turned forty when we met. She didn't seem to want children and that was an attraction and a relief for me. She took the oral-contraceptive pill and I used condoms, and our sex life was afforded a safety zone for experiment and enjoyment. But the more I got to know her sexually the less I felt I knew her in other ways.

I started to look at places Irene and I could go for a holiday within my price range, but other events soon took over. My parents both went into hospital on the same winter's day, a show of togetherness suited to a marriage of nearly fifty-three years. I took a computer and clothes to my parents' home in Staffordshire and lived there for four months. Seven weeks into my stay my father died; I was now a father without his child and a child without his father.

My mother, suffering from a stroke and multi-infarct dementia, was discharged from hospital three days after my father's death. I returned to Oxford whenever I could, and Irene sometimes visited me in Staffordshire at weekends. One Thursday night in Oxford, four weeks after my father's death, Irene and I greeted each other with enthusiasm and energy in my flat.

'Are you busy over the weekend?' I asked her, when we lay together on the Friday morning.

'I'm going to Paris today to see the Matisse exhibition,' she said.

'Oh, that's a shame. I was hoping to spend time with you.'

'I'll be back on Sunday night.'

'Are you going with anyone?'

'Well, Ivan will be around.'

'In Paris?'

'Uh huh.'

'Oh.'

I didn't sleep that Friday night. My head was swimming with losses. My father had died, my mother had gone into an altered state, and I sensed that my almost-live-in girlfriend had drifted into a different life. Ivan was separated from his wife and family, and Ivan had obviously taken a real interest in her.

That Saturday evening I went to a party and talked to one or two people about my emotional discomfort. Their advice seemed to fall into two camps. One group thought I should ask Irene to leave and the other group thought I should collect together all her possessions and toss them out into the street.

Of course I did neither. I struggled along for a while before realising that the relationship with Irene couldn't work. Then she moved out.

Irene and I saw each other occasionally over the next few months. Then a traumatic incident caused a watershed in my life. It triggered another review of my role as an absent father. It happened after a weekend that I'd spent with Irene in London. Afterwards nothing would be the same for me again.

Back in Oxford after our weekend together, Irene came round to my flat after work

'Ivan's on a life-support machine,' she told me. 'He's overdosed.'

I held her for a while but I found it very difficult.

'I'm not sure I'm the best person to support you on this one,' I said. I didn't have enough sympathy for Ivan…or Irene.

A few days later the life-support machine was switched off and Ivan died.

Six months later a depression tied me to my bed for two days. My life froze and I could hardly eat. Then I remembered Ivan and energy returned to my body. This was something to do with Ivan. I needed to find out more about Ivan.

'I've read obituaries of Ivan and collated a list of his published writing,' I told my friend Trudy a week later, trying to explain my new obsession.

'So what next?' Trudy asked. We'd known each other as platonic friends for eight years. She knew me well and I respected her intuition. She had a soft, gentle, soothing voice that instantly healed me. She had also grown up in the town where my birth son's adoption order had passed through court 25 years earlier. Trudy knew my birth-father story.

'I'm going to read through Ivan's work because I think there's something about his life that seems important to me,' I said. 'I think it's because his career was one that I might have had if I had stuck to my earlier direction. I feel driven to understand him more.'

'Do you feel responsible for his death?'

'A little. I was wishing he wasn't around and then he kills himself.'

'Didn't you say that his life was in a mess?'

'Yes. His death was probably more to do with his life. He'd been in and out of hospital the year before he died. While I was with Irene on the weekend of Ivan's death her phone rang and went unanswered. I sometimes wonder if it was him calling and what might have happened. But that might have made things worse for him. I don't know what I'm doing now though. It seems odd to find myself obsessed with a dead man I've never met.'

We fell into silence. Mostly Trudy and I spoke on the phone. This time we were face to face, drinking tea in her home. She lived in a detached house. It was the only Oxford house I knew where you could drive a car off the road and into a driveway.

'It's your pattern,' Trudy said.

'Eh?'

'Your pattern.'

'How do you mean?' I asked.

'Your loss. A boy is born and then he disappears before you meet him. Then you start searching for what you can learn about him.'

Aha.

'So Ivan comes into Irene's life and then he disappears before

I've met him?' I asked. I thought some more. 'My birth son comes into the birth mother Carol's life and then he disappears.'

'Could be.'

'So what I should be doing is learning about my birth son?'

'That's one explanation,' said Trudy.

'It's all there, isn't it?' I said, after thinking it over some more. 'That distance between Carol and me is what Irene and I had at weekends when she was in London.' I pondered some more. 'And it went on for about nine months between her and Ivan, and then he died.'

'Or got adopted.'

'So I've started searching for all the information I can find about Ivan.'

'Whereas really…'

'It's about my birth son.'

'When you're ready.'

'I wish I could solve the adoption issue.'

'Hey, we all do what we can.'

Here was my pattern. I had a continuing theme of either mistrusting women when they were in other towns or choosing women who should be mistrusted when they were in other towns. Or in some subtle way I encouraged them to stray.

My pattern was one of loss. I had lost a child and never recovered from it. I had lost women and been devastated by break-ups. I needed to do something about the root cause.

Three years later I met Louise Archer for the first time.

3

Summer 1997

'How did you get on with the search for the file?' Louise asked.

'Not very well,' I said. 'I wrote to Adoption and Fostering at the two most likely Social Services departments. Both agencies replied to say that they didn't have the file.'

'Really?'

'I got a letter from one of them. It's from the Service Development Manager: *I can't find anything relating to the above named and wonder whether there are any other names that the child could have been known by. I've also checked the child-in-care files, but there is no trace.'*

While Louise went into a thoughtful trance I looked at her more closely. The setting was the same as for our first meeting. She was wearing brown trousers and a beige cardigan over a white shirt.

'I feel emotionally exhausted already,' I added.

Louise got up and took the Georgina Stafford book from her bookshelf – *Where to Find Adoption Records.*

'The files should be with the county council you've approached,' Louise said, after she had thumbed through the book. 'I can't see why they don't have anything.'

She looked through her papers and took out one sheet.

'Here's a list of national agencies,' she said, handing me a sheet of paper. 'You probably need to write to them as well. There's a chance that the adoption might have gone through one of them.'

I looked at the names on the list – Dr Barnardo's, Children's

Society, NCH Ashwood Project, Father Hudson Society, Family Ties, Christian Family Concern, Childlink, Caris, and so on.

'Write again to the two most likely Social Services,' said Louise.

'Again?'

'Would you like me to do some of that on your behalf?' she asked.

'No, thanks. I need to do it. I want to feel that I'm doing something.'

'And write to some nearby Social Services.'

She gave me two more addresses.

I said, 'Years ago I spoke with a woman from an adoption organisation and she told me that boys usually search later than girls.'

'Yes. Boys don't always search themselves. The wives often do it for them. Women are better at saving articles out of magazines, ringing for numbers, etc. The wives are more likely to find the national contact register or NORCAP.'

'That was the name – NORCAP.[1] Remind me what that stands for.'

'The National Organisation for the Counselling of Adoptees and Parents.'

'Yes. I joined NORCAP when he was eighteen. But I'm not on the national register.'

'You probably need to be named in the file to get on the national contact register.'

'Yes. I think that was what they told me.'

'OPCS General Registry Office,' Louise said, without consulting anything. 'Adoptions Section, Smedley Hydro, Trafalgar Road, Southport.'

'That's right. I tried to register with them, but they wouldn't take my registration because I didn't have proof of paternity.'

'Yes, you need the file first. But you may not be named in the

---

1 Now known as NORCAP – Adults Affected by Adoption – a UK registered charity to help adults with search and reunion issues.

Social Services file so you can't necessarily get confirmation of paternity through that route either.'

Confirmation of paternity.

Maybe that was what I was seeking.

'I've been registered with NORCAP for about ten years,' I said. 'Wouldn't he be most likely to go through that route?'

'He may not know to contact them, but NORCAP are the most obvious organisation for adoptees to approach if they are thinking of a reunion.' Louise pointed a finger at me. 'NORCAP wouldn't tell *you* if they had a match; they'd just give the information to the adopted person.'

My mind was buzzing with ideas. Carol's parents had been involved in the adoption; could I get more information from them? I could write to them asking if they would forward a letter to Carol. Or maybe I should wait until I have a clearer idea of where he is. But what if she'd met him already?

The thought of meeting Carol again made me shudder. I looked around the room and noticed a box of tissues within my reach. I ignored them for the moment.

'What else can I do now?' I asked.

'I think working on finding the file is enough for now. Later I will explain about other things I can do.'

'And discover his new name?'

'Yes. That's our plan.'

I thought about Carol, her parents and her other family. I thought about my parents, the adoptive parents, their other family members, the whole amoebic labyrinth that existed around my birth son. I remembered an expression my father had learned during his World War II army days: *You can only go as fast as the slowest vehicle in the convoy.* I quickly understood that my search would be like that. There would be lots of stopping and starting, watching and waiting.

'Now let's talk a little about your piece of writing,' Louise said. She had picked up some papers. 'Let's talk about Irene.'

'Uh huh.'

'You make the two triangles very clear,' Louise said. 'There was Irene, Ivan and yourself. And there was your birth son, the birth mother and you. In both cases you had a dyadic relationship with a woman, conducted at a distance for part of the time, and then a male person came into her life, another male competing for her love.'

'One was an adoption triangle, the other was the eternal triangle.'

'That's what I'm trying to get my head round.' She picked up a book from the table by her left hand and showed me the cover.

'*The Adoption Triangle*,' I read. 'Is that what we are talking about?'

'No, it's not,' said Louise. 'It's not your adoption triangle. The classic definition of the adoption triangle consists of the child, the adoptive parents and the birth mother. No sign of the birth father.'

She stood up, drew various triangles on her blackboard. I stared at them for a long time. I looked at the one showing Carol, her parents and the child. Then I looked at the one showing my mum, my dad and me.

'I was excluded from most of the triangles,' I said. 'That's how the adoption felt.'

'In adoption literature birth fathers are generally seen as feckless and fly-by-night characters. But that's not been my experience when I've met them.'

'It's affected me deeply.'

'I can tell.'

I looked again at the blackboard until I sensed my place – or lack of place – in all the triangles. Louise let me think.

'My adoption triangle should be birth mother, birth father and child,' I said. 'I need to think about this some more.'

'It's very confusing.'

We went quiet.

'I completed my other homework task,' I said, finally. 'I wrote down six motivations for my search.'

'Well done. Shall we go through them?'

'Yes, please.'

I found the place in my notebook.

'They are not in order of importance,' I added.

'OK,' said Louise. 'Number one?'

'To make it easy for him to search without fear of rejection.'

'Good.'

'I think it makes much more sense for the birth parents to instigate contact. The birth children may fear a second rejection if they take the initiative.'

'Correct. But could we talk about him as an adopted person rather than as a birth child, please. He's long past childhood now. He will be approaching thirty. Number two?'

'To complete the narrative.'

'Meaning?'

'I know so little of the full story. I don't know who he is or where he is. I don't know if he is still alive. I don't know his name. It's a story with no end. It's a novel with only the first chapter. I'm constantly inventing endings for the story. I'd like to know the real ending.'

'Number three?'

'To ensure that he has access to family history and medical history if he ever wishes to know it.'

'Yes. Four?'

'To free up my life so I can decide which direction to take. So much of my career is tied up with surrogate searching.'

Louise nodded.

'Next reason?' she asked.

'I need him to know he's never been forgotten.'

'Yes. That's important. In my experience all birth parents remember sons and daughters who were placed for adoption, but the adoptees don't necessarily know that. And your other reason for searching?'

'Who else might be interested in my family pictures except for him?'

'OK. Well done. Put those somewhere safe and you might wish to go back to them on occasion. Is there anything else?'

'I suppose I don't expect to fully understand my reasons until afterwards. Maybe I need to prove that it really happened because it's a bit of a dream really. Overall I just feel driven to meet him.'

'The big worry for adoptive parents is that they might feel pushed out.'

'I don't want to hijack a son now that they've done the hard work of rearing him. I'm a loner. I'm an outsider. I was told long ago that the best I could hope for was to be a friend of my birth son.'

'What if you are not his original father after all?'

'I'm fairly sure I am. If I'm not, then I guess he would end up with five parents – two adoptive parents, two birth parents and me.'

'That's good work on your reasons for searching,' Louise said. 'Can I ask you another question?'

'Please do.'

'After that incident with Irene it took you three years to decide to meet me. What was happening in the meantime?'

'I think I was trying to clear the space in my life for the search. There was a lot I needed to get out of the way. I decided to leave Oxford and move to the north and that meant I had to deal with a lot of change before I was ready to move the search forward.'

'Do you have enough support for what you're doing?' Louise asked.

'I have you, Louise, I have a lot of close friends who know my story, and I have a search buddy.'

'A search buddy?'

'Yes. Her name is Nan. She is searching for her half-brother and I am looking for my birth son. We made a pact to be there for each other during our searches.'

Louise nodded. I took it as approval.

'You've moved closer to your roots, haven't you?' Louise asked.

I thought about her question. I had moved closer to where I had lived as a teenager, nearer to my birth son's birthplace. I thought

I was moving away from Oxford because Oxford was crowded, expensive and polluted. I thought I was making a rational decision to move to a relatively inexpensive town in the Peak District with a rail station, a swimming pool and fresh air. Subconsciously I was not moving away from Oxford but moving towards Louise Archer, moving towards my birth son, confronting my search.

Louise Archer smiled at me, so I continued.

'My mother was ill for a long time and then she died,' I said. 'With both parents gone I felt more free to search. But first I had to deal with their house and a lot of possessions. And the idea of searching felt very demanding. It wasn't until I went on a trip to the United States earlier this year that I realised I could create the strength to do the search. While I was away a few significant things happened. When I came back I contracted with myself to try to search.'

'Contracted?'

'I sat down and wrote a contract to myself and signed it.'

'You seem very committed.'

'Yes. The things that happened while I was away were quite powerful.'

'Can you tell me about them, or would you prefer to write them down?'

'I'll write them down. It helps me to get things straight in my own mind.'

'OK. I'll look forward to reading about your trip to the United States.'

'That may be the nearest I'll ever get to being a travel writer.'

4

A contract to search

A month before my trip to the United States I made a phone call that kick-started my search. It was the first time I had ever knowingly spoken to another birth father.

'Is there anything I can do to find out who my birth son is?' I asked.

'Yes, there is,' he said. 'There are ways and means. But you need to be patient. Prepare for peaks and troughs.'

He explained a few things I could do and I listened attentively.

'You must involve a mediator,' he told me. 'I can give you the name of an independent intermediary.'

'Yes, please,' I said.

I wrote down Louise Archer's number in three places.

'Isn't it illegal to search?' I asked.

'No. For years I thought it was, but that's what they want you to think. There is no law saying that you can't do the tracing. Any adult can approach any adult. Birth parents signed away parenting rights – not all rights – and parenting rights end at eighteen. The only potentially illegal position would be if someone harassed an adopted person after receiving a refusal. That would come under harassment laws. But I've never encountered any legal problems.'

'For years I've assumed it was illegal and the adopters had all the power.'

'The adopters have the power. It's just that they may be infertile.'

'Thanks for that. I feel better now.'

We laughed.

'You've been a great help,' I said.

'I found my daughter and it's brought me a lot of happiness,' he said. 'If I can help anybody else I'd be happy to do so.'

We ended the call and I was left tearful by the telephone.

Maybe that was the moment I turned from a passive birth father to an active one.

My American trip provided many surreal moments. In New York City I met a woman whose grandmother was a hundred and four. In California I met a man who was deliberately cranking up his weight so that he could leave the army. In Oregon I met a woman who'd had two children by the same father – one before they were married and one after they were divorced.

In the fourth week of my trip, I was riding on the 5.07pm Coast Starlight train from Eugene, Oregon, to Oakland, California, when I tried to squeeze my rucksack into an overhead luggage rack. My back twanged and seized up. It wasn't a total surprise; a lifting injury a few months earlier had caused intermittent suffering and fearful back spasms.

As the train travelled through the night I lay on the floor in the restaurant car. When it got to daylight, a kind conductor took me through to an empty sleeping car where I could at least lie down. At 9.20am the train reached the end of the line. The conductor organised an electric vehicle for me and I was embarrassed at being given a lift from the platform to the station concourse.

In the train station I found a public telephone with a *Yellow Pages* directory. I tracked down the nearest chiropractor and made an immediate appointment. It took me some time to get into the taxi. Then I gave the driver the chiropractor's address.

The chiropractor worked alone. He invited me through to his treatment room and asked me to stand on two sets of scales. I put my right foot on one and my left foot on the other.

'You're badly antalgic,' he told me. 'One side of your body weighs thirty pounds more than the other.'

I could see that was a problem.

The chiropractor talked as he worked.

'I've had a very English morning,' he told me. 'There's just been an English writer on the radio. A mystery writer.'

'Male or female?'

'Male. Lives in Oxford.'

'Colin Dexter,' I said.

'That's the guy.'

As he treated me, the radio news summarised the previous night's Academy Awards and the success of *The English Patient*. I came out of the treatment room nowhere near fit. I needed to book into a motel.

'Please use the phone,' the chiropractor told me, pointing to his reception area. 'There's a phone book here.'

I made an appointment to see him again the next morning and thanked him for his help. He returned to his treatment room.

Then I noticed the woman who was to change my life. She was sitting in the waiting room reading a magazine. She had fair-to-ginger hair and was about my age.

'Are you English?' the woman asked me, when we were left alone.

'I am,' I said.

'I lived in Oxford for a time when I was a young woman.'

'That's where I've been living.'

'Try the Ramada,' she told me.

Then the chiropractor called her through. The woman turned to me.

'Wait here,' she said. 'I can give you a ride to your motel. I'll only be five minutes.'

Five minutes later, she came out of the chiropractor's office laughing.

'I'm parked just outside,' she said, chuckling away as we headed for the door. 'Let's put your bag in the trunk.' She carried my bag to the car.

I took forever to fold myself into the passenger seat. She must have felt very safe with me. I was incapable of assaulting anyone. I could hardly move. But she was still laughing.

'What's so funny?' I asked at last.

'Oh, you know that film that won all the Oscars last night – *The English Patient?*'

'Yeah, yeah, the chiropractor had it on the radio. We were talking about it.'

'Yes, well, he's calling you The English Patient.'

I laughed.

'Yes, of course he would,' I said.

'Did you see *Secrets and Lies?*' she said, suddenly, mentioning a film that had been nominated for five Oscars alongside *The English Patient*. 'That was an English film, wasn't it?'

'Yes. A Mike Leigh film.'

'Did you see it? Did you like it?'

'Yes, I saw it, and thought it was very well done,' I said.

Secrets and Lies tells the story of a young black woman who searches for her birth mother after the death of her last adoptive parent. One thing that struck me was that adopted people are released from some of their loyalties when their adoptive parents die. Similarly I felt that I had more freedom to pursue my search now that my own parents were dead. But the search for my birth son still felt too emotionally demanding. After one small act, like going to see *Secrets and Lies*, it would take me weeks to recover.

Now I looked across at this American woman, side-on, saw the pain in her face and decided to continue to the next level.

'I had a personal interest in *Secrets and Lies*,' I added.

She looked across at me.

'So have I,' she said.

Yes, of course she did. We'd both given up children for adoption.

She drove me to the motel and carried my bag to Reception.

'Take an upstairs room,' she advised me.

Memories of a thousand California motel-room murders came

back to me from reading mysteries by Raymond Chandler, Ross Macdonald and the like. She carried my rucksack to my room. Then we went out to find sustenance.

It was a sunny day in paradise, barely 11am, but she needed an alcoholic drink in a bar. I had a sense of her living on the edge, needing a smoke, a drink, drugs, body comforts.

We went for lunch and started telling our stories. We were born within three days of each other and our birth sons were born five days apart. Our fathers had both had careers in professional sport and we'd both tried to write our fathers' stories. We talked in great detail. I was very uncomfortable while sitting so we went back to my motel.

In the motel room we lay on the bed together.

'Have you actually seen *Secrets and Lies*?' I asked.

'Not yet. I haven't been able to face it.'

We talked for a while and then she took off most of her clothes and got into bed. I took off some of mine and struggled into bed next to her. I had taken painkillers but I was still incapable of any sudden movements. Throughout the afternoon we continued with our life stories. We held hands and kissed shoulders. Mostly we talked openly.

Here was one of my problems in relationships. The connection could be too quick. It was immediately intense and intimate, it was contaminating and claustrophobic. This was not a normal start to a relationship. It was not 'Fancy a game of cards?', 'Let's catch a movie' or 'There's a good show at the Comedy Club tonight'. Instead it was 'What's the most traumatic event of your life?' 'Have you seen a movie about that trauma?' and 'Let's undress our bodies and minds and let our grief come forth'.

As we shared our lives I learned several things. I found out that we came from different cultures – in her case the birth father had served in Vietnam – and we started from different positions in our loss. She didn't feel she could ever try to trace her son and there was other trauma in her past.

We agreed that the adoption decisions had been about keeping up appearances and our parents' fear of scandal. We had been left with so much to overcome while so young. We felt we had every right to be angry – at our parents, our in-laws, our governments, the adoption agencies. I wanted to make life easier for her. I wanted to take her to see *Secrets and Lies* and then comfort her afterwards.

We talked about books. She recommended *The Stranger Beside Me* by Ann Rule, two books by Peter Matthiessen (*The Snow Leopard* and *At Play in the Fields of the Lord*) and the work of Mary Summer Rain, who she described as 'easy reading and hard thinking'.

We talked about our previous relationships.

'I was at a party,' she told me. 'This man walked into the room and I just knew he'd be the love of my life. Have you ever had that?'

I went through my relationships like scrolling a computer file.

'Sort of,' I said. I realised that I had incredibly strong images of my first sight of certain women, including Carol, the mother of my birth son.

'He was the person who came into the room, came into my life, and made such an impact,' she said.

We talked and talked and gently rubbed against each other for eight hours. Then she went home to her other life.

Three weeks later I travelled on a train between Hartford, Connecticut, and Boston, Massachusetts. I sat bolt upright, my head high, staring straight ahead, trying to retain good posture to give my back every chance to recover further.

Two young men sat in front of me. One was reading a computer magazine that was full of programming code and computer jargon. I found it difficult to read the magazine over his shoulder and sensed that I wouldn't have understood it anyway. The magazine was just a meditation point for me while I was busy trying to balance my body. Then the young geek turned the page and a new headline blew gustily down the train carriage and slapped me in the face.

ONCE LOST NOW FOUND

Sixteen years after she gave up her baby boy, one young mother went looking for him online and encountered a Web of adoption resources.

When the train arrived at Boston South Station I bought a copy of the magazine. On the green line train to Newton I read the article about tracing adoptive relatives. A number of American organisations were listed in the article, including Bastard Nation and American Adoption Congress. The sub-editor had pulled out one quotation so that it stood alone: *That evening, Qualls went to a movie. When she returned home she logged on once more and saw a new email message. She read: 'Is this for real? I'm your son.'*

Adoption had been following me around like an experienced private detective and finally I had spotted the tail. I resolved to be proactive. I decided I had to follow it up. I had been close to giving up and burying the episode for ever. Now, after talking to a birth father, meeting the woman in California and seeing the magazine on the way to Boston, I had new resolve. This is something that I have to do, I thought. I can't ignore the signs. I must solve this adoption riddle. I must trust myself to cope with everything that might arise. But I wasn't convinced about the internet route. It seemed too sudden, too dramatic, too invasive. I had a feeling that someone could get hurt.

While travelling in the United States I sometimes wondered if the loss of my birth son had stopped me from emigrating at various times of my life. Maybe I kept returning to England because I didn't want to be too far away from him. This time, when I arrived back in my home country, I made a contract with myself to search for my birth son. In my absence from his life this was about the only fatherly thing that I could do. I might have been passive in other ways but I could be active in the business of searching. I already knew that it would be the hardest thing I'd ever done. I would have to be dogged, committed and patient, and I needed healthy boundaries.

I typed out my contract and signed it.

5

Autumn 1997

'Any luck with finding the file?' Louise Archer asked me, after we had taken up our customary positions.

'No,' I said. 'As soon as I got home I wrote to fifteen national adoption agencies and changed my address with NORCAP.'

'And nothing?'

'I've probably heard back from half of the national agencies. I wrote to some other counties near where the baby was born.'

'Did you try the two most likely ones again?'

'I did. I phoned the Service Development Manager at the county council I'd approached a few months ago but she was away on holiday for a fortnight, so I wrote a letter with my request.'

'Did you hear from her?'

'Yes, she wrote back when she returned from holiday. She said they didn't hold the file a few months ago and they still didn't have it now. Or words to that effect.'

'That's odd. The file must be somewhere. There are one or two places where records were destroyed by fire but it shouldn't affect where we are looking. The file should exist.'

'I searched for the address of the most relevant court, and rang the court to find out which area they covered.'

'And?'

'Nothing except my emotional exhaustion. I began to wonder if my birth son would have the same trouble finding his own file.'

'It may be clearer to him from the documentation his adoptive parents were given. How about writing to the Service Development Manager again?'

'I've approached her twice already,' I said.

'Try her again. Ask her if it could have been misfiled.'

I sighed. Was it going to be like this all the way through? Fighting through barriers. Going over the same ground.

'Keep trying,' Louise told me. 'Don't lose heart. This is what it's like.'

'I'll do it,' I said, eventually.

'Well done.'

'Thank you.'

'And thanks for writing about the trip to the United States.' She reached for a few sheets of paper. 'I read your travel stories. I liked your synchronicity of the woman in California. I can see how it has put searching on your agenda. I've heard a lot of those coincidence stories and I think they go with the adoption territory.'

'It sent a strong message to me.'

'I got that impression. I was also interested in the article in *Yahoo! Magazine*. Do you still have it?'

'Yes. Would you like me to photocopy it for you?'

'Yes, please.'

'I feel as though I need to be getting on with something while I'm trying to trace the file. I need other tasks.'

'OK. You could look through the electoral registers in the region covered by the court. Look at the registers for eighteen years after his birth.'

'Will I need to go to the local libraries for the back issues of electoral rolls?'

'Yes. It will take a few phone calls to find out which library holds them for that area. If you look at the electoral rolls for eighteen years after his birth, you'll be able to find birth dates of youngsters who turned eighteen during that year. They have to list the birth dates of eighteen-year-olds; if there's an election before their eighteenth birthday they can't vote, if there's one after they can. See if you can find your birth son's exact date of birth in those lists. Make a list of the names of those with that date of birth. Then they can be checked against the adoption registers for the year of birth. There's not many people with dates of birth against their name but a lot of pages to go through.'

'And some parents would have moved from the area.'

'That's right. There's probably a fifty-fifty chance that the parents were still in the same area when he turned eighteen.'

This conversation triggered my memory. I tried to capture some more fragments of the original story. I remembered that Carol had told me that the child had been fostered for six weeks and was then formally adopted through a court at six months.

'There are ways and means but it needs patience,' Louise told me. 'Steel yourself for highs and lows.'

'Anything else I can do?'

'Yes,' she said. 'You can go through the adoption registers at the Family Records Centre and list those with the same Christian name as the one he was given by his birth mother. That name may have been kept as one of his Christian names after the adoption. The adoptive parents may have chosen their own favourite name for him and then turned the original name into a middle name.'

'So I make a list?'

'Yes. Then we can call up adoption certificates for those born around the right time.'

'Good.'

I was excited now. There were things I could do and Louise was sounding more like a detective.

'Let's get the information and then we can talk through what the next step may be,' Louise said. 'When we next meet we can talk about whether we need to call up any adoption certificates. I have a system in place for ordering certificates.'

'Great.'

'I think it would be worth writing to the court, too,' Louise told me, 'just to check that the adoption did go through there.'

'How did that system work?' I asked.

'When the adoption papers went through, the birth mother

received confirmation of the adoption order. This came through quickly after the court hearing. Most were within six months. Write a letter to the clerk of the court, saying "I understand my son was adopted through the court." Give them the full name and birth date and ask if they could confirm it. That would at least confirm that he was adopted there. They could have been intending for him to go to one area and then it was switched at the last moment.'

'Great,' I said, without meaning it.

'A lot of birth mothers didn't understand what was happening,' Louise said, after she had given me some background on guardian ad litem reports and mother-and-baby homes. 'They just filled in the forms. They didn't say, "Wait a minute" or "No". They just went along with it.'

I nodded. In the late-1960s the age of adulthood was twenty-one. Carol was still under parental control.

'There's one other thing I've been meaning to say about your writing,' Louise said.

'Yes?'

'You write about your *birth son*; why do you refer to him in that way?'

I was puzzled.

'Because I don't know his name,' I said, thinking it was obvious.

'No, I mean, why *birth son*? Why not just *son*.'

'Oh, I see. Well, that's how we are known in the adoption business, isn't it? I'm his birth father and he's my birth son.'

'Yes, but we can still call him your son. My feeling is that you are doing that because you don't feel you've earned the right to call yourself his father. It feels a bit like self-punishment to call him your birth son.'

'Oh.'

'It's like you're hanging back.'

'Yes.'

'It's just something to think about when you're writing.'

'I'll do that.'

'We also need to talk about Christmas,' said Louise.

'Oh, it's good of you to invite me.'

Louise wagged a finger at me.

'No,' she said. 'I was going to say that I don't do any intermediary work in the four weeks before Christmas or the month after. It's too difficult a time for people with adoption issues.'

'Yeah, I hate Christmas.'

'Is that something you might want to write about?'

'Yes. That will give me something to do over Christmas.'

'Family losses come up at Christmas.'

'Yes,' I said. 'They do for me.'

'Let me know how you get on with the library work. Please don't go racing off. Don't try to do too much. A little bit at a time.'

'I'll write something about what Christmas means to me.'

'And maybe your feelings around his birthday.'

'Oh, yes. I'll write about his eighteenth birthday. Now that's a story.'

6

Anniversaries

Christmas was always a difficult time for me, year after year after year. I wanted to do something unconventional during my university Christmas vacations. When I saw that waiters were required by an elite Peak District hotel (with accommodation provided) I decided that I would happily spend three weeks working. I travelled for four hours through thick fog for an evening interview but I didn't get the job because I had a beard. 'Some of our customers are quite conservative,' the manager explained.

Another year, when working as a milkman, I was delighted to work over Christmas but that was no reason to stay a milkman all my life.

Every year I would get a phone call from my parents towards the end of summer.

'Are you coming home for Christmas?' my Dad would ask.

'Can I think about it?'

'Of course. You'll have to think quick though because we'll need to book the restaurant.'

I loved my parents dearly, loved the grandmother figure who joined us for Christmas Day, and was happy to see them at other times of the year. At Christmas I found myself wanting to avoid my family and ignore the media razzmatazz. I didn't want to make myself miserable with months of not looking forward to a family Christmas when part of our family was missing.

I've always sensed that among the jollity of Christmas there is plenty of quiet desperation. People stop work and get ill, and marriages break up. Christmas in modern society is not a restful time. It can be a jumble of parties, long-distance travel and family intensity. I yearned for peaceful escape.

I shared Christmas with my parents every other year. In between I experimented with alternative Christmases. I connected with other childless people, husbands estranged from their wives and people whose families were overseas. I enjoyed spending Christmas Day on my own in quiet contemplation. I envied a friend of mine who told everyone that he would be away for Christmas and then drew the curtains and stayed home.

I met a university student who had a similar disregard for festive spirit. Together we concocted a list of twenty 'how to avoid Christmas' tips. They included escaping to a Lundy lighthouse, crossing the international date line early on Christmas Day, finding a Buddhist retreat, adopting a capricious diet that makes you impossible to cater for, wearing earplugs in shops to block out festive carols, and attending an assertiveness course to practise saying 'I have a right to decide how I want to spend Christmas'.

I disliked Sundays too. Sunday seemed a designated family day. As a freelancer I usually worked on Sundays and viewed it as just another day. Bank Holidays were even worse than Sundays for me. I have been known to turn up at a library on a Bank Holiday Monday only to find the library closed. Bank Holidays were 'Blank Holidays' to me.

The seasons of the year give rhythm to our lives. I noticed aspects of the spring and summer when people were out enjoying family activities and fertility rites. My childlessness could be a problem then, but generally I learned to avoid places where there were children. I babysat only under protest. I never changed a nappy.

Another bad time was the annual build up to my son's birthday. The few days leading up to his fifth birthday were particularly bad. It was during my second year as a mature university student and I hit a sudden wall. I'd completed all my term's work, read through my pile of extra-curricula books and was wondering what to do next, rudderless without a schedule. I was normally well disciplined at university but now I found myself lying in bed like a growing teenager. I could do some light reading but I found it difficult to engage with the world. It was a few days of depression.

This became a pattern. Every year a period of subtle heaviness would arrive for a few days before his birthday and it would be harder to get out of bed in the morning. Then I would remember that the despondency had a cause. It was the impact of a birthday that was missing several people, without birthday cards and minus birthday presents. I was burdened by grief as I subconsciously counted the number of candles on an imaginary cake. The depression lifted when his birthday passed. Then I returned to normal, whatever normal was.

I was almost always aware of his age. During his childhood I was concerned about him when I read about teenage criminals and missing children. I was enthused to read about school sports teams. But when tragedies occurred, when a young person died, I felt it more acutely than the people around me. It was especially hard if a young male of around my son's age was a victim of sudden death. A tiny item on an inside page of a newspaper could get me thinking Is he still alive?

In the year before he became eighteen I started a relationship with a woman called Valerie. This was a real watershed in my fatherless life. During the period Val and I were together, off and on, hot and cold, chalk and cheese, the loss of my child coursed through my body and battered my insides. Something just as formative lashed out within her.

We were in our late thirties when we met. She was slim, lithe and world-weary. Her long red hair was a traffic stopper but I should have seen it as a warning light. She was such a fervent feminist that she read only books written by women. I met her because she was a hairdresser in her spare time. She started by cutting my hair and then remodeled me. She advised on new clothes, took off the beard I'd had for thirteen years and swept my hair away from my forehead. She forced me to see my real face in the mirror.

Valerie was attractive, entertaining and comedic. At first she called me Mr Hugger but later she called me all kinds of names. It wasn't long before we touched each other's vulnerable points. One night about two months after we'd started sleeping together her mood swung dramatically and suddenly. One moment she was amenable and the next she was trapped in a box of anger banging against the walls. She raged at me about something I couldn't understand. On the surface it was something to do with me not ordering a taxi until they were all booked. Deep down, I now know, it was about our losses. In one corner of the boxing ring was Her Loss; in the other corner was My Loss.

Valerie's biological clock was ticking softly and chiming loudly. She was desperate to have a child and I was subconsciously avoiding one because my first experience had been so traumatic. Ours became a volatile relationship. We were trapped in mutual tension. I was considered good father potential but my deep wound stopped me from going too close to fatherhood. By now I had cut myself off from the high-paying careers of my twenties and early thirties so my finances felt too shaky for rearing children.

I wrote about this period in my notebook: *My son reached eighteen this week but I have never met him. Of course I don't really think of him as 'my son' because he was adopted. I think of him more as a child I sired, unknowingly, in those pre-abortion days when women had no right to choose…I never saw the son I fathered eighteen years ago but I may meet him soon. It is his right. Not mine. I think about it all occasionally, never quite sure of his birth date, and for years unsure of the emotional impact it was having as it tugged away at me. Quite simply, my first experience of childbirth was a bad one – guilt, difficulty and legacy, something that needed to be worked through before I could face up to it again and enjoy it.*

It all welled up for me now. He was on my mind a lot more. And I knew I needed help. Some of my spats with Val showed me that I was far from calm inside. Also, I'd heard that the law had changed, allowing adopted children over eighteen contact with their birth parents if they so wished.

I started my research by phoning the local Social Services department. I was put through to an adoption-and-fostering social worker. She came straight to the point.

'It's very important to consider the effect that it has on the adoptive parents and the child's needs,' the social worker told me. 'Things should be done through writing. That gives people time to gather their thoughts.'

'Would the adoptive parents know my name?'

'Not normally, though in some circumstances they may.'

'So am I likely to have someone turn up at my door in the next few weeks?'

'A lot of adopted children don't take the opportunity. Most want to know where they came from. Thousands do search.'

The social worker gave me the address of the National Organisation for the Counselling of Adoptees and Parents (NORCAP), which was based in Purley, Surrey. She was careful to point out that NORCAP was not a tracing agency.

A short time later NORCAP moved to a new office in Headington, Oxford, a ten-minute walk from my workplace. Adoption stories are full of such coincidences.

About five weeks after my son's eighteenth birthday I visited the new NORCAP office on a Saturday morning. I spoke to one of the workers, breaking off while she handled incoming telephone queries. I was in the office for an hour.

She told me the child would have been registered under the mother's maiden name. Social Services may have my name or they may not.

'Did you give your consent at the time?' she asked.

'I don't know,' I said. 'I think I filled in forms and met with someone. I can't remember who she was.'

'To register with us you will need his exact date of birth.'

'I may need to check that. How do I do that?'

'You need to get a birth certificate from St Catherine's House or the registry office local to where he was born.'

'Right, I'll do that,' I said. 'Could you tell me something about what to expect. Might he be getting in touch with me soon? I hear the law has changed.'

'The law was not changed, only amended, allowing adopted adults access to their original birth certificates.'

'I see.'

'Very few children start the search at eighteen,' she told me. 'Lads in particular. I sometimes worry if youngsters do come forward at eighteen. There's usually something wrong if that happens. Girls on average start in their twenties, usually when they are married and have children of their own. The fellows generally start when their babies are little toddlers or when their wives grow interested. They are older than the women when they start to search – generally late twenties, or thirties or even their forties – and a number of them won't do it in the lifetime of their adopted parents.'

I didn't know whether to be disappointed or relieved.

'They need to be independent,' the NORCAP lady continued. 'Think about it, and you'll realise that during their early twenties male children are busy pursuing their careers and trying to establish themselves.'

I thought about it. I knew what she was talking about because I was working part time as a careers counsellor in higher education. Most of the people I advised and counselled were between eighteen and twenty-one.

Aha.

This was the 'aha' moment when I first realised the deeply subconscious nature of my search. Why was I working as a careers counsellor? Was it because I had the right skills for the job or was it because an eighteen-year-old was missing from my life and I wanted some connection with him during his university years?

'A lot of men go to the mothers first,' the NORCAP lady said, after taking another phone call. 'It's a logical thing to do if the father's name is not on the birth certificate. There can be problems if mothers give the wrong name for the birth father at the time of the birth. They feel that if they give the real name they might not be able to get the lord of the manor as their husband. The trouble is, when the named men are traced they are nothing to do with it.'

During a lull, while the lady answered a phone call, I thought about the term she had used – *birth father*. It was a new term to me. For over a decade I had thought of myself as a biological father.

'The adoptive parents had the right to change Christian names as well as surnames,' the NORCAP lady told me. 'You can't know the adoptive parents' names.'

'Would the biological mother know?'

'No,' she said. Then she paused. 'Well, sometimes people read upside-down at the time. But they are not necessarily aware enough to remember.'

During the next telephone break I checked my notes. One key thing to arise from my discussion with the NORCAP lady was that feelings of curiosity and loss needed to be satisfied. Mothers never left behind their feelings of guilt.

'The boy will feel better than you do,' said the NORCAP lady, when she ended the call. 'He'll feel better if he finds you and better that he knew you cared enough to register with us. But the birth parents will be mourning the loss of a child and the child will return as an adult. The best you can be to him is a friend rather than a father.'

'I'm starting to sense the conflict between the interests of the adoptive parents and the real parents,' I thought aloud.

'That needs to be treated sensitively. Given a stable enough upbringing, however, the child can have his cake and eat it.'

Before I left I purchased a book of family reunion stories from the NORCAP lady and spoke to her about how the stories were written up.

'Are these fiction stories or nonfiction stories?' I asked.

'Real stories with the names changed.'

I went home and read the reunion stories. I cried at the gateway to catharsis.

For thirteen years I lived in a garret flat in Oxford. The building's ground floor was occupied by a factory social club, and an Aunt Sally alley clattered noisily on Wednesday evenings. You went up forty-six steps to the top flat and the final flight of stairs was at such an angle that you felt you were sliding into the stairwell.

The flat had potential but it had had potential for thirty years. There were curtains from the fifties, wartime utility furniture, dodgy electrics, a gas fire in the living-room and a gas fridge in the kitchen. A pile of old wall calendars could be recycled every five years, six years or twenty-eight years. The previous occupant of my room had moved out after half her ceiling had collapsed and wrecked her stereo system. The flat was ideal for a struggling writer like me.

During my thirteen years in the flat there were six ceiling collapses and several blockages of the kitchen sink. Countless tiles skittered off the roof to give the pigeons open access. The neighbours rehearsed for rock-band gigs and bits of plaster dropped off the walls and the ceilings. One visitor said that the only two decent things in the flat were a blue-and-white vase and the door out. But I thought that this was how an aspiring writer had to live.

One day during my relationship with Valerie I told my two flat-mates that I had a son who'd been placed for adoption and I might get a call at some time.

'How does the system work?' one flat-mate asked.

I explained what the NORCAP woman had said. As I was speaking, the doorbell rang.

'That's probably him now,' my other flat-mate said.

We all cackled.

Then I froze a little. I could feel the shock coming on. What would I do if it was him?

It wasn't.

Relief.

Val and I broke up and then reunited six months later. We talked more about having a child together. I felt as though I would have to give up my writing career if I were to earn enough money to support a family. I was offered a more secure job but it was in the wrong town at the wrong time. Val didn't want to move away and I didn't blame her. By now she was approaching forty.

There was still a lot of anger in our relationship. We went to see a marriage guidance counsellor and that brought everything to a head. We had two joint sessions and then Val went on holiday with some women friends. The counsellor offered me a session on my own.

'Yeah, it's you who needs to go anyway,' Val said.

I met the counsellor alone and saw it from my perspective. I clearly didn't want to be in a relationship with Val. It was stressful to end the relationship and leave her but it was also stressful to stay in the relationship. I eventually realised that I had to tell Val that it was all over. I dreaded the moment when I broke the news. As it turned out, I was quite right to dread it.

We were in the bedroom of Val's house. She sat on the bed showing off her holiday suntan. It was the first time I'd ever seen her wearing a skirt. She looked very attractive but I now thought that she needed a father rather than a lover.

'I went to the counsellor on my own, as you suggested,' I told her. 'I talked it through and thought it over, and I decided that I want our relationship to end.'

She didn't take the news very well. She got to her feet quickly and swung her right hand at my face. I saw her CND badge catch in the light as her second right hook glanced off my protective hand and cut my lip. I covered up better when I realised I was in a fight but quickly found a way to leave the room, leave the house, leave the relationship. I didn't even feel like fighting back.

If a partner hurts you physically it is not a sign of caring. But I had to take responsibility too. I had let myself get involved in something damaging to me. I was still punishing myself for what had happened all those years ago. I might as well have been beating myself up rather than let Valerie do it.

Val soon took up with another man. I saw them together in the pub across the road from where I lived, typical of the way we had been baiting each other. A month or so later she was pregnant by the new man; at least I assumed it was by the new man. The dates were a bit tight.

Eventually she phoned me.

'Hello,' I said, answering the call.

'This baby I'm having,' she said, speaking through clenched teeth. 'It's not yours.'

'Oh. Thank you for telling me.'

She hung up.

'Good luck,' I told the dead phone.

A few months later I was in a pub with friends after we had watched an Adrian Lyne film called *Fatal Attraction*. Some of the scenes between Dan Callagher (Michael Douglas) and Alex Forrest (Glenn Close) reminded me of being with Valerie. What started as sexy suddenly turned dangerous.

My friends were generally critical of the film.

'The mother thought the girl was five and the father thought she was six,' said one.

'Why didn't he tell his wife sooner?'

'What do you think the film's message is supposed to be?'

'Don't cheat on your wife in the era of AIDS.'

'The moral is that you can do anything to people but don't touch the dog or the rabbit.'

I didn't say anything. I identified with Dan Callagher, except that I didn't have a wife or a dog and I wasn't raising children.

7

Winter 1997–98

I travelled for over two hours to visit the library that held the relevant electoral registers. I looked at the year he turned eighteen. I was inside the library for three hours and missed lunch. The library was crowded and noisy as building work was going on all around. The girl next to me was wading through Kompass Directories. People came to read the daily newspapers. Two people chatted to each other about local accommodation.

I thumbed through the registers looking only for birthday dates. I noted those born on the day of his birth and those born within two days (just in case the adoptive parents had the wrong day in mind). The first three people born on my son's birthday were all female. Then I found a male with exactly the right birth date but his name was Jamil Nawaz. I wouldn't have minded my son having an ethnic name; I just assumed that the church adoption agencies of the 1960s were not that liberal and therefore this wasn't him.

Names came and went – hundreds of them by the minute. I saw my own name was listed. I saw Debra and Deniece. The names rolled by like wagons on an everlasting goods train. And then I found a male with the right date. Made a note of his name. Here was a chance. Could this be him? It gave me heart. Stick to it, I told myself, go through the rest.

Every half an hour I forced myself to get up and walk around for a few seconds. Every few minutes I looked into the distance and did my eye exercises. I was very aware that my eyesight was deteriorating. Earlier that week I'd read a football result as 0-0 only to discover two days later that it was 6-0.

There were four female names – Julie, Jennifer, Elizabeth and Wendy – with the correct birth date. Surely none of them could be him. Surely adoptive parents would not have been so cruel to give a boy a girl's name. I tried to remember when the Johnny Cash song 'A Boy Named Sue' had been written. Was it before or after my son's birth? I thought for a while and then stopped noting the girls' names.

At the end of my three-hour shift I was left with two possible candidates – males who had turned eighteen on the same day of the same month of the same year as my son would have done. I looked at the electoral rolls for the year of their birth. Both families were there. One seemed an unlikely candidate because there were too many other names listed at the address (possibly older siblings). But just in case one of these two names was the right one I traced the families up to date through registers and telephone directories. One family was still at the same address. The other had moved on six years previously. I put the two names on a list for further investigation.

Could he be Michael or Nicholas?

I felt as though I finally had some power. But I ended the day with a severe headache.

Another time, passing through London, I spent an hour at the Family Records Centre in Myddleton Street with a list of tasks. Some were straightforward family history queries. Others were related to the search. First I turned to the two names I'd found in the electoral registers, eighteen-year-olds who should be exactly the same age as my son. I looked in the adoption register for those names. They weren't there. I had done all that work for a dead end.

I looked through a few pages of the adoption registers, searching for adopted people with a Christian name the same as my son. I sampled a few pages and realised that it would take me hours. I promised myself I would return when I had more time and energy for the task.

I also looked for Carol's married name. I found that and quit while I was ahead. I had something to report when I met Louise again.

At times when I seriously considered giving up my search, just when my resolve was exhausted, a coincidence would dutifully appear in order to spur me forward. One winter's day an acquaintance invited me for a walk with her dog Meg. She brought along a friend of hers. The stranger was a fit young woman who was well versed in the local terrain and its folk history. I thought she might have a background in geography or anthropology.

'What do you do during the week?' I asked.

'I work in Adoption and Fostering,' she replied.

She didn't need to say anything more. She'd already fulfilled an important role in my life. She had reminded me that I should keep my search moving forward. James Redfield's book *The Celestine Prophecy* was all the rage at this time. According to the first rule of the book, we had to accept our coincidences and recognise that they were there for a purpose.

I received a letter from the American woman I had met at the chiropractor's in California. She had finally watched *Secrets and Lies* and found it painful. It was the story of her family, she told me, the story of her family's motto ('The less said the better'). She rued our friendship being based on common loss. We had no way of knowing what our relationship could have been. Our lost children had interfered.

In my local library I picked out a telephone directory and checked the last address I had for Carol's parents. Over twenty-five years later they were still at the same address.

I drafted out a letter to Carol's father. I felt that I needed to warn him that I was trying to resolve my personal issues. In my draft letter I thanked him for encouraging me to get a better education and talked a little about what I had been doing since. Then I couldn't find a way of ending the letter. I never turned my draft into a completed piece of work. I never sent the letter.

I made a note of his phone number instead.

I spoke to Louise Archer on the phone.

'Did you write again to the most likely Social Services?' she asked me.

'No. But I haven't been idle. I spent some time at the Family Records Centre assessing the task ahead. I will plan a day there the next time I am in London.'

'I understand. Take it at your own pace. Let Christmas disappear further into the past.'

'Will do.'

'I felt for you when I read the story about your son turning eighteen,' Louise said.

'Thank you.'

'A lot of birth parents think that their offspring might suddenly turn up when they reach eighteen but it's quite rare.'

'Looking back I was ridiculously optimistic.'

'It's understandable to be optimistic. The eighteenth birthday is an important rite of passage. But an eighteen-year-old is usually living at home and the last thing they want is more parents. Why would they saddle themselves with *more* parental control?'

I laughed.

'Good point,' I said.

'But the eighteenth birthday is a hopeful time for birth parents and their emotions take over,' Louise said.

'True. But it's not a good time for the eighteen-year-olds.'

'There was one other thing I wanted to follow up,' Louise said.

On the phone I was listening more closely to Louise's voice. Her accent belonged in another county.

'What's that?' I asked.

'It was the piece in your account of the NORCAP meeting,

where you say that birth mothers can deliberately give the wrong name for the birth father.'

'Yes?'

'Well, I don't think that happens very often. Back in the 1960s I think a lot of birth mothers had a very good idea who the father was. They weren't promiscuous. If they got it wrong it was because they genuinely believed it was the other person who got them pregnant.'

'Thanks, Louise,' I said. 'What's my next writing assignment?'

'I've been thinking about that too.'

'Yes?'

'The first time we met you mentioned that the adoption has affected your career choices. Then again, in your passages about his eighteenth birthday, you mentioned about you being a careers adviser around the time that he was eighteen. Were there other ways it affected your work?'

'I'm sure there were. I think I have been subconsciously searching through my work ever since the event happened.'

'Could you write about some examples?'

'I could try. I think the adoption event has turned me into a writer and researcher of a particular kind. I'll go through my CV and see if I can find the surrogate father in me.'

'And write to that Social Services department again if you can face it.'

'I'll try.'

8

Career choices

During my university vacations I travelled as much as possible. When my son was six I went to Canada. At the ferry terminal in Argentia, Newfoundland, I met a Yale University sociology student who became a lifelong friend. Manny Ramos was a 6ft 5in Cuban-American with shoulder-length hair and a big beard. He wore a check shirt, jeans and a parka coat. With his sunglasses he looked very cool. I'd recently read James Michener's *The Drifters* and Jack Kerouac's *On the Road*, and now Manny helped me to lift my travel career off the page.

I found his dissertation particularly interesting. He'd hitchhiked around North America doing a follow-up study of seventy street friends and acquaintances he'd known six years previously. He told fascinating tales of tracking down his subjects. He'd drunk smoothies in Hawaii, had two accidents on the Alaska Highway, interviewed a prison inmate, and followed a painted trail up a Colorado mountainside to meet one drop-out. Mostly, though, he had met his subjects in suburbs and middle-class districts. Seventy per cent of the former drop-outs were now going straight as teachers, truck drivers, law students, nurses, newspaper reporters, trades people, managers and so on.

After travelling with Manny for a few days I became very interested in his work. I sensed the value and allure of what he was doing – it was the most fascinating project I had come across at that point in my life – and I wanted to do that sort of longitudinal study (as we sociologists called them). Subconsciously, there was one six-year follow-up narrative that I particularly yearned for.

In my late twenties and early thirties I did some freelance work as a consultant statistician. My brief was to study the diffusion process of products in the pharmaceutical industry. According to traditional wisdom, customers adopted new products in different ways. The first to adopt were the innovators, followed by the early-adopters, late-adopters and, eventually, the laggards. This was the product-adoption process.

There was that word again: *adoption*.

I couldn't escape it.

My statistical consultancy work grew so the word *adoption* came up more and more. It tripped off my tongue regularly as I researched the adoption of pharmaceutical products but I didn't make the inductive leap to the adoption of babies. My boss moved from Cambridgeshire to Oxfordshire and then offered me a full-time job. I turned down his offer but moved to Oxford anyway and worked for him as a freelancer for three or four days a week. Increasingly, however, I realised that I got the most satisfaction and pleasure from simple activities that came cheaply: writing, reading, walking, running, watching, talking and loving. I also realised that if I was going to write books I needed to have tight financial control. I saved money by making jam, beer, wine and bread.

Then I got the part-time job as a careers counsellor in a Student Services department. There, I dealt with students of similar age to my son, studying them one by one, trying to make sure that I treated them kindly as I didn't know who might be part of my family.

Was he the one who'd had a summer job carrying a sandwich board along Oxford Street?

Was he the lad who'd worked in a Spanish bar last summer?

Was it him who'd sold ice cream on a beach in France?

Or was he the youth with a stutter who wanted a career in broadcasting?

Outside my work there were lots of other chance encounters that could also have involved my son.

Was he the hitchhiker I picked up at a five-way intersection in Suffolk?

Could he be the young lad in the local greengrocery who made me laugh with his repartee ('Cucumber – eat here or takeaway?').

Or was it his voice that I heard at the Open University when I phoned with a query?

Having a birth child is a great exercise in imagination. No wonder some birth parents turn to writing. The whole adoption scenario is like a feed for a creative-writing exercise.

Then one day my imagination worked overtime. I thought I'd found him...

As a careers counsellor I worked in an office without outside windows. It was built from partition walls. I knew I had an appointment at 3pm that day but first I wanted to deal with a wasp. I chased the wasp for five minutes. He went into the standard lamp so I switched off the standard lamp. He went into the strobe light so I switched off the strobe light. Then he went into the small piece of window over the door. I plucked a newspaper out of the bin and dealt with the wasp with some finality.

I composed myself and looked at the form that my next student had completed in advance. His name was Colin North and he was from the town where my son's adoption had gone through the court. He was aged nineteen – the right age – but we didn't ask students to state their birth date on the form so I was uncertain about his exact age. I was very nervous when I went outside and invited him into the office.

I no longer had my beard so I felt more exposed. Did Colin North look like me? Well, he certainly had the same number of ears. That was about as far as I could go.

Colin North was doing an HND in Computer Studies. At his age I had done a part-time HNC in Mathematics, Statistics and Computing. My God, he was me. He came from the right place, was the right age and had the right career. I started to convince myself that there was a likeness. I almost shook with nervousness.

Could this really be him?

'Have you had careers interviews before?' I asked him.

'One at school.'

I waited for him to go on. He did eventually.

'A bit of a waste of time,' he said. 'They didn't know what to say.'

He curled up his lip. He was a shy, embarrassed youth. Just like me at that age.

'Have you got ideas now?' I asked. I was always interested in why they had come to see me at this particular point. Sometimes it was because their parents had sent them.

'I'm thinking about doing a degree,' said Colin North.

We talked about the course options and where he might do the degree. I explained how to get more information about courses and colleges. We worked through what sort of degree course would suit him. I gave him some literature. I asked him if he had any other concerns about doing a degree.

'I'd be quite old and all my friends will be working,' he said.

'Does that bother you?'

'It hasn't so far.'

He would be going to university late. Just like me. Could it be him?

I continued by asking the questions that I would normally ask. I showed him how to appraise his own skills. Then we looked at the longer-term scenarios. What sort of career did he want eventually? Did he really need a degree to do that? Would a degree offer him more flexibility? We talked about computer programming and how to get jobs. We talked about other careers. We took a general look at the labour market.

We were well into the interview when I had good cause to ask him the question I'd been desperate to ask. We were talking about grants to do a degree.

'When will you be twenty?' I asked him.

He answered. It was the wrong answer by six months. It was the wrong boy. I didn't know whether to be pleased or sad. But when I got home I wondered if he had gone to the same school as my son.

Were they in the same class?

Did he know him?

Had he been to his house?

The incident with Colin North prompted me to seek a birth certificate for my son. Over a year had passed since my meeting with the woman from NORCAP and I still needed to confirm the details of my son's birth. It prevented me registering with NORCAP.

When I clarified my son's date of birth I learned that I was a day out with what I thought was his birthday. He was registered under the mother's maiden name. The space for the father's name was left blank and I thought this was particularly bizarre. Here was one of the most important things in my life, if not the most important, and it was represented by an empty space. I was invisible to the world. No wonder I felt ignored at times. No wonder I whispered my body language.

I told my friend Trudy about finding the birth certificate.

'You could easily be a grandfather,' she told me. 'You were a father at his age.'

I shuddered at the thought.

'Can you be a grandfather if you've never really been a father?' I asked.

During the latent odyssey of searching for my son there had been long periods of normal functioning. To all intents and purposes I was living a stable life. I was having a laugh. I was doing well in jobs. During most years the loss of my son affected my functioning only in the period before his birthday and around Christmas. But his eighteenth and nineteenth years had been different. During those two years he had been omnipresent in my life, forcing his way to the surface of my consciousness.

After five years as a careers counsellor, I became a full-time freelance writer. It took a while before I became aware of the metaphor of writing books and making babies. I've sometimes taken nine months to write a book. At other times, like an elephant, I have taken two years to get the book outside of me. Occasionally one of my books has been a fifteen-year project, like raising children to their teenage days. The publishing process added to the metaphor; I could hand over a manuscript and then, perhaps nine months later, a baby book was born.

Often I can remember the moment a book is conceived. An idea and a resolve to go forward stands out like the moon in a clear countryside sky. Maybe, after the adoption, I was more determined to complete writing projects. My life was complex and chaotic in many ways but when it came to writing I had discipline and self-motivation.

9

Spring 1998

I sat at home looking at a list of sixty-seven adoptees with the same Christian name as the one Carol had given our son. Could one of these sixty-seven be him?

I had just returned from a London trip. While in London I'd freed up an afternoon to go through adoption registers at the Family Records Centre. I'd noted down all the adoptees with the correct Christian name. Back home I'd arranged them in order of volume number and entry number. This didn't quite coincide with the chronological order that they passed through the courts but it was a start.

I stared at the list and tried to interpret its meaning for me. Ultimately the adoptive parents had the right to change all Christian names but a few might have kept the original name as the second or third name. What would be going through the minds of the adoptive parents? Surely the choice of Christian names would depend on their surname. Many names would need to be changed to fit the new surname. The original might be rejected because it could have created awkward pronunciation (Felicity Fazackerly), too specific a meaning (Victoria Cross) or a difficult acronym (Brenda Ursula Moore). Or the original name could have been rejected because it would duplicate initials already in the family and they didn't want mix-ups when the post arrived. Or the new parents had chosen Christian names years before they discovered that they couldn't get pregnant. Maybe they had a family name they were committed to.

I've referred to 'Christian names' and 'original names' but I've also heard them called forenames, first names and given names. The adoptive family had the option of changing names, so my son's original moniker could have been a given-and-taken-away name.

I stared again at the list of names and tried to find a clue. In five cases the Christian name I sought was shown as a stand-alone name. In two cases it was the first name of three. In seven cases it was the second name of two. In the other fifty-three it was the first name of two (and in nearly a quarter of these the second Christian name was the same each time).

What did it all mean?

I spoke to Louise Archer on the telephone.

'It's just to keep you informed of developments,' I told her. 'I've not yet traced the file even though I've written to more adoption agencies. And I've thought more about where Carol might be.'

'Did you write again to the most likely Social Services?'

'Yes, I finally plucked up courage. At least I could address my letter to a specific person.'

'Well done. I know it's going over the same ground but you never know. There's something odd about it all.'

'I also visited the Family Records Centre in London,' I said. 'I made a special journey this time and I've compiled a list of adopted children with the same Christian name as my son. If his sole Christian name had been retained then he would be down on this list.'

'How many names?'

'Over sixty.'

'That's not too bad.'

'It's better than twenty thousand.'

'I think most have their original names changed,' Louise said. 'In this case I think the odds are against them keeping it. I think it's one of those love-hate names.'

'Yeah, you're probably right, but I need to call up a few adoption certificates just to make sure. How long do you think the system would take to record an adoption?'

'It would vary. About six months on average?'

'Right. Let me give you two names.'

I read out the names and reference numbers.

'I'll order those adoption certificates for you,' Louise said.

'Thank you.'

'And thank you for writing about your careers.'

'I felt such an idiot that I'd made a mistake with my birth son's date of birth.'

'Your son's date of birth,' Louise corrected. 'Please don't feel bad. It's quite normal for birth parents to get the date wrong.'

'I bet birth mothers don't get it wrong.'

'Oh, they do. They can even get the year wrong.'

'No? How can they forget that?'

'It's quite common to be confused about it all in the wake of the shock. It's part of the coping mechanism for dealing with the trauma.'

'I suppose some birth mothers never mention the date of birth again after that.'

'They may have been told to forget everything about the event.'

I received a letter from my contact at the most likely Social Services. She was now called Adoption and Specialist Placement Manager rather than Service Development Officer. She wrote me a kind letter listing all the places she had checked with no result, and I thought it was more bad news. But when I continued reading I learned that she had gone down into a dirty, musty basement and checked the minute books of the local diocesan. There she'd found a single line entry saying the adoption had been transferred to a nearby county. She said she would contact the other county and see if they had any records.

'Yesssssss,' I said aloud. I was getting closer to the file.

I read the rest of the letter from my wonderful new friend, the Adoption and Specialist Placement Officer: *I will come back to you*

as soon as I have any further information. I'm glad to have been able
to locate something for you.

I wrote to thank my new buddy. I wrote to Louise to tell her
that the file had been moved to another county. Louise had been
correct all along. Keep pestering them, she'd told me.

'I'm sorry,' Louise Archer told me, speaking on the telephone. 'I've
called up those two adoption certificates and they're clearly the
wrong ones.'

'OK, thanks for trying.'

'I think the odds are very much against his name being
retained.'

'Even if Carol asked for his name to be retained?'

'Yes. The name can still be changed.'

'Could you give me all the different dates on the certificates so
that I can get a better guide as to how the system is working.'

'I'll do that.'

'Thank you. Can we order two more?'

'If you wish.'

I carefully chose two more adopted people who had my son's
original Christian name, people whose birth date might be nearer
his. Louise stayed on the line.

'I read about your working history,' Louise said. 'What are you
writing at the moment?'

I laughed heartily.

'Touché,' I said, when I'd thought about it. 'Guess what? I had a
number of work options but I made a classic subconscious decision
– I chose to work on a follow-up study. I'm tracing and interviewing
graduates from up to twenty years ago.'

'Simulating the search for your son again.'

'Yes, of course. My real research project is a thirty-year follow-up
study. I may need your help tracing a few of the graduates, by the
way.'

'I'm here when you want me.'

'It was really helpful writing about my career.'

'I think it's understandable that you are looking for him in the street, wondering about the others of a similar age, trying to be nice to them, just in case there was a connection.'

'It wasn't as though every person of a similar age set off the trigger. I think it needed a combination of factors. Maybe I was more sensitised to the loss near his birthday or around Christmas.'

'Yes, I understand,' Louise said.

'Those writings have helped me to see myself more clearly. Underneath the surface I'm a damaged parcel, Louise. My imagination has tossed me around the sorting-offices of the world, trying to get myself delivered to an unknown address, and I've no longer got any wrapping-paper on me.'

'Oooh,' said Louise.

'So what's my next writing task?'

'There was something else I wanted to ask you,' Louise said.

'Please do.'

'You once said that you were what is *called* a birth father,' Louise said. 'Does that mean you don't like the term birth father?'

'Correct. It makes me feel like I should have been there at the birth and yet I wasn't. It adds to the guilt.'

'What would you like me to call you?' Louise asked.

'Call me Andy,' I said.

'Ho ho. You've also used the term biological father. How did you think of yourself after the adoption? Did you have a name for yourself?'

'Probably the bastard who fathered a bastard.'

'Besides that.'

'I think I first heard the term birth father when he was eighteen and I went to see the NORCAP lady.'

'I don't think the term existed in the 1960s or 1970s.'

'The first time I had a name for myself was when I fell in love with a beautiful woman in Kentucky. My son would have been about seven at the time. Ruby had been adopted but her real mother was a distant relative of her parents. Ruby referred to her real mother as her *biological mother*. I liked that term. For years I thought of myself as a biological father.'

'You also used the term real mother then.'

'Yes. I guess I'm a real father. I've recently joined the Natural Parents Network so I'm also a natural parent.' I thought about it. 'I'm a natural parent but parenting has never come naturally to me.'

'There are lots of terms for you,' said Louise.

'I've also heard blood father and genetic father. What are the others?'

'Original father. Hereditary father. Putative father.'

'What's a putative father?'

'A putative father is the one commonly supposed to be the father,' she explained. 'It's a term that often turns up in social work files. Did you meet an adoption social worker at the time of your son's birth?'

'Yes,' I said. 'I remember answering questions about eye colour and interests and the like. The adoption decision had already been taken.'

'There are some strange terms around adoption,' she said. 'Reunion is fine for a birth mother and her birth child, but it isn't always relevant for birth fathers and their birth children.'

'It can't be a reunion without a union in the first place.'

'Exactly.'

'I suppose I could only have a first meeting with my son.'

'That's what we're working towards.'

'Thank you.'

'What happened to Ruby?' Louise asked.

'Ruby started as a one-night stand but stayed in my life. She helped me understand my life as a biological father.'

'I think I'd like to read about Ruby,' she said.

'Coming up next.'

10

Ruby

I woke up from a hazy sleep at 1pm on the day I met Ruby. My bedroom was a Greyhound bus travelling from Lexington to Louisville, the moving wallpaper was the rolling hills of the Kentucky landscape and my alarm-clock a man having an epileptic fit in the seat behind me.

'Hey, driver,' shouted a man further back. 'Stop the bus, this man's having a seizure.'

It took a while to sort that out.

The bus arrived in Louisville, Kentucky, at 2pm on the day of the Kentucky Derby. I left my rucksack in a Greyhound bus-station locker and walked along Third Street. I had never seen such a quiet city on a Saturday. Signs showed that everything was closing at 4pm. Placards said WELCOME RACE FANS. I went into a shop and bought a copy of the *Louisville Times* (Derby edition) for 15 cents.

'Am I going the right way for the racetrack?' I asked the shopkeeper.

'Sure thing,' the shopkeeper said. 'About three miles thataway. Past the U of L.'

'What time's the big race?'

'The Derby?'

He pronounced it Durby.

'Yeah, the Derby,' I said. I pronounced it Darby. I knew it was pronounced Darby because I'd lived in Derby, England.

'Five thirty,' the shopkeeper said.

I set off for the door.

'Come back now,' the shopkeeper said.

I turned round and walked back to the counter. The shopkeeper looked shocked. I learned later that it was just an expression: *Come back now. You all come back now.*

I walked four miles along Third Street to Churchill Downs racetrack. The weather seemed very British. I put on my jacket, took off my jacket, all the way there. I went around the perimeter of the racetrack and studied the street sellers as they packed up their stalls. I saw people watching from the roofs of nearby houses. I spotted piles of rubbish. Then I saw Ruby for the first time. She was a Latin American beauty with short bushy black hair and brown skin. We walked towards each other, smiled and slowed.

'Do you know how to get in with this ticket?' she asked me, in her Kentucky drawl. She showed me the ticket. 'A guy's just given me this.'

"This is a grandstand transfer ticket,' I said, looking at the ticket, looking at her. 'I think this just allows you to go to a different section of the stadium when you get in. You have to pay ten dollars to get in first.'

I had already decided not to pay the entrance fee.

'I've just paid three dollars to park my car,' she said.

'Let's walk to the far end. I have a feeling that something is happening there.'

'OK.'

She bought a soda from a street-vendor, came back with two straws and offered me a drink. After that we hardly took our eyes off each other.

'Are you English?' she asked.

'Does it show that much?' I said.

On our walk around Churchill Downs Ruby told me about her bad day. The previous evening she'd finished her nursing shift at 11pm and driven her battered Volkswagen to a night-club called The Toy Tiger. She'd broken up with her boyfriend, left the night-club alone at 4am and crashed her car on the way home. Getting home at 6am, she'd tossed and turned and cried in bed. Rising in the morning, she'd prowled the apartment and then gone back to bed. When she woke up in the early afternoon, she'd found a message from her room-mate asking her to meet a group of people at the Kentucky Derby. Ruby hadn't wanted to go anywhere but the apartment had felt too quiet.

'It'll be hard to find your friends in a crowd this big,' I told Ruby, as we walked around Churchill Downs towards where a small crowd was congregating at a locked gate. One man was reading the odds through binoculars.

'Can we get in here?' I asked the others.

'Yeah, this is for the locals,' one said. 'They'll let us in after they sing My Old Kentucky Home.'

'This is my twentieth Derby,' said one local, pronouncing it Durby.

'It's my thirty-fifth,' said another.

'It's my first,' I said.

Ruby laughed. Her face lit up.

The gates were opened just as the big race was about to start. We ran across the open space and watched the Kentucky Derby for free.

After the race Ruby and I waded through the infield. It was a mass of debris. There were discarded leaflets, empty cans, used newspapers, cigarette ends, Kentucky Fried Chicken cardboard and drug paraphernalia. Ruby and I stayed close to each other. We hung back from the crowds as they jostled towards the exit.

'This makes me think of the Ibrox Stadium Disaster,' I said.

'The what?' she said.

I explained about how sixty-six people had been killed at Ibrox Park, Glasgow, in the last few moments of a soccer match in 1971. Many Rangers fans were on Stairway 13, leaving the ground, when a roar from the crowd caused people to change direction and a crush occurred.

Ruby looked at me intently.

'You know, you look like Dan Fogelberg,' she told me.

'Who?' I said.

'Dan Fogelberg. He's a singer-songwriter. He has a beard and long hair too.'

Ruby and I had a lot to learn from each other.

We walked among the crowds towards her car.

'Anyone want to buy a NO PARKING sign?' asked a man holding a road sign.

'No, thanks, already got one at home,' someone replied.

Ruby took me back to her apartment, where half a dozen people were partying.

'Do you want to rest?' she asked midway through the evening. We both did. It was during our time in her bedroom that I discovered she had been adopted as a baby. Her real mother lived over a thousand miles away, a distant relative of her parents. Ruby saw her very occasionally and called her 'my biological mother'. She didn't know who her biological father was because her biological mother wasn't sure.

Ruby gave me a name to call myself – I was a biological father.

She gave me my family identity.

I stayed two days in Louisville and then returned to the Canadian university where I was studying for a Master's degree. Ruby and I exchanged long letters. In her second letter she revealed that her father was terminally ill and would not live more than a year. When a friend of hers invited me to spend the summer in southern Indiana I accepted the invitation. I wanted to be close to Ruby.

Ruby and I spent much of that summer together. She nursed her daddy and nursed patients at work. We partied when we could, went to the zoo, and made love to Starland Vocal Band's Afternoon Delight. I worked on my MSc thesis and read everything I could find about the Kentucky Derby, including Hunter Thompson's famous piece of gonzo journalism. For me the race meant a summer of adventure, sex, writing and, as ever, sadness. I was a biological father with someone else's adopted daughter.

I was belatedly living a hippy's life. My hair had a year's growth, my beard was a bird's nest, and I wore a red T-shirt saying REVOLUTION IS THE OPIATE OF THE INTELLECTUALS. But I knew I would return to the nine-to-five world at some point.

I wanted to stay with Ruby through her daddy's terminal illness. My visa was running out but I found a job as a statistician just across the state border in Indiana. I saw a lady in the Louisville naturalisation office and she seemed positive about my staying in the country, but the naturalisation office in Cincinnati, Ohio, told me it was virtually impossible for me to take the job. I would have to spend months out of the country completing the paperwork and the employer would have to prove that no American citizen could do the work. Even if Ruby and I decided to marry I would have had to undergo months of paperwork back in Britain. So I left the United States.

'Keep on truckin',' Ruby and I told each other.

Ruby's father died four months later. Then Ruby and her momma moved to a new beginning, a long way from Kentucky. Ruby left no forwarding address for our mutual friends in Kentucky. She dropped out of sight but never out of my mind. And Ruby didn't ignore the past for ever...

Ruby's phone call came from nowhere, fifteen years after we had parted in difficult circumstances. My son was now twenty-two, the same age as Ruby had been when I'd first met her. She'd phoned my parents for my telephone number before leaving a message on my new answerphone.

When I collected her message I got gooseflesh at the sound of her Kentucky accent: *Hi Andy, this is Ruby. I just spoke to your Dad and asked for your phone number. That's an interesting answering message you have there. Well, let me give you my phone number. I'm living in Annandale, Virginia, and it's seven-zero-three-two-eight-zero-two-five-five-five. That's my home number. And I'll try to reach you another time. I understand there's a time difference. Being Saturday I'm in and out today. My friend and I are coming to*

England in May and I wanted to talk to you about that. And I want to see how you're doing. I'll talk to you later. 'Bye.

I listened to the message four or five times and relived our whole experience. Then I calmed myself and phoned her number.

'Thanks for getting in touch,' I told her when we spoke. 'It's wonderful to hear your voice.'

'I kept on transferring your folks' address from one address book to another, thinking I may use the number eventually,' she said.

'I'm pleased you did.'

'I'm coming to England with my friend Judy,' she said.

'When?'

'June.'

'Would you like to meet?'

'I would love to.'

Over the next few weeks we caught up on our last fifteen years via a series of letters and photographs. After her father's death Ruby had moved with her adoptive mother to a new beginning but life had been difficult with a string of unsatisfactory relationships. In Florida Ruby had taken up snow skiing, motor-bike riding and hard exercise in a gym. When she hit thirty she became 'real serious' about her life, taking courses at a nearby university, then doing a degree and changing career from nursing to interior design.

'You met me in my brain-dead years when my hormones were open to almost everything,' she told me in one of her letters. 'You were one of my better life experiences.'

That really surprised me. I had always felt guilty about abandoning her when I returned home from the United States. I'd always felt I'd been a bad experience for her.

Fifteen years after I'd last seen Ruby I stood at the ARRIVALS section of Heathrow Airport and watched the people come past in their hundreds. I saw small children run to their grannies, lovers fall into each other's arms, and husbands kiss their wives quickly before asking for the car keys. I grew more and more nervous every minute. Would I recognise Ruby now that her hair was long, thick, curly and a third of the way down her back? Would she recognise me without my beard and long hair? A delay increased my tension. I was enormously excited. I was so thrilled to be waiting. Then she was ten yards away, walking towards me, whispering 'Aindy' and opening her arms for the inevitable embrace.

In England Ruby and I reprised our Kentuckiana summer. She was on vacation, I took a rare break, and we spent much of the time together. We went to Oxford, Bath and Stonehenge. I took her to my parents' cottage in Staffordshire. I showed her pubs, colleges and Roman ruins. We stayed in cottages and my writer's garret flat.

We talked about our adoption experiences. She spent more time with her biological mother these days. She was now fairly sure who her biological father was but couldn't contact him.

Then Ruby went back to her life in Virginia. Eighteen months later it was my father who died. Ruby and I had played out our relationship in reverse.

After that we stayed in touch. Soon after Ruby's visit, she hooked up with her future husband and I met Irene.

11

Summer 1998

Louise Archer phoned me to say that there was no joy from the next two adoption certificates.

'I bet they've changed all his Christian names,' she said.

'Possibly,' I said. 'Let's try three more.'

I read out the certificate numbers and she said she would get to work.

'Look, there's something else that we could try,' Louise said. 'It's a bit of a long shot but I should tell you about it. I can't tell you too much about it but it's about the trail of official records that follow the birth.'

What followed was an elliptic conversation. It took me some time to grasp what she was alluding to and what she wanted me to work out for myself.

'So when a child is born,' I said, eventually, 'surely the birth contributes to the start of a lifetime of medical records? Is that what you're saying?'

'Uh huh,' she said.

'Any complications in the birth have to be recorded,' I said.

'Do they?'

'I think there was a complication in our case.'

Suddenly, out of nowhere, I remembered Carol's blood group. It was an unusual one. Was there a way to trace a child through the mother's blood type?

'So maybe the National Health Service number was changed?' I said. 'Or maybe it wasn't? There has to be a link inside the health service somewhere.'

'I know someone who knows someone.'

'Maybe the NHS numbers are changed to protect the identity but not always.'

'Shall I make an inquiry?'

'Please do.'

I wrote to Ruby in the United States and told her that I was searching for my son.

Ruby wrote back: *If my biological father found me I'd welcome the opportunity to get to know more about him and my heritage. I would question him about his motives and 'Why now?' just to get into his head. Being adopted however has never been a source of angst or anger for me. It's a non-issue and that's not true for some others. I wish you well and be brave.*

Another coincidence followed. I answered an advert in a regional magazine – WOMAN SEEKING MAN – and had a nice telephone chat with the woman who'd placed the advert.

We met outside a theatre a week later. In a nearby café we talked for half an hour before she asked the key question.

'Do you have any children?' she said.

No, I thought, preparing my answer. Then I looked into her face. Again I saw a person's painful smile. I had been on both sides of that smile and here it was again.

'I have a birth son,' I said. 'He was adopted immediately after he was born.'

'That happened to me too.'

We shared our stories.

She owned her decision more than I owned mine. The age of adulthood had been lowered to eighteen and she had been able to give the matter more rounded consideration. The adoption system had changed by the time of her child's birth a few years after mine. The 1970 Houghton Report had recommended counselling for parents surrendering their child for adoption.

The woman became a friend rather than a lover. Maybe it was better to avoid romantic complication in favour of family resolution. My search was verging on the obsessive, thanks to the scale of the task, the lack of official support and the difficulty of solving the locked-door mystery. Each small step required tremendous emotional energy and I wanted to keep some reserves in case a large step suddenly appeared.

'I'm sorry, the medical records didn't lead anywhere,' said Louise. We were speaking more often on the phone these days.

'You did say that it was a long shot.'

'And nothing from the next three adoption certificates. None of them match your son's date of birth.'

'Could you give me some details from those three adoption certificates, please. I'd like to become a statistician again.'

She read out the figures I wanted. I thanked her and we said goodbye.

At my desk I studied the registration process for the seven adoptions represented by the certificates Louise had called up. They had taken between 167 days and 241 days to go through the system from birth to adoption certificate. I was beginning to realise that delays could have occurred at various points in the administrative system – the court, the original local registrar and the general registrar.

I calculated the standard deviation for the whole process and worked out that 95 per cent of the adoptions would have gone through in 148 to 260 days.

I phoned Louise again.

'There are four more I would like to try,' I told her. 'Then I'll call it a day with this idea.'

The cost of adoption certificates was beginning to encroach.

'OK, I'll order them up,' she told me. 'But I still think his original Christian name would have been changed.'

'I think you're right,' I said.

I received a letter from the adoption social worker in the Social Services department that held my son's file. She confirmed that I was named as the putative father of the child.

Putative father?

Louise had prepared me for this term.

I was a biological father, birth father, blood father, genetic father, hereditary father, natural father, original father, real father and putative father.

I hope this will enable you to register on the Adoption Contact Register, the social worker wrote. *I am unable to provide any court details of the adoption. If you should wish to leave a letter on file for any future date that he might contact this agency please send it to this address for my attention.*

I spoke to her on the phone.

I learned that any letter I sent would be read only by the adoption social worker, whose job was to forewarn children in case there was anything upsetting in the file.

I had located the file but I felt even more downcast. I knew that Louise Archer was on my side. But whose side was the social worker on?

The phone woke me from a long and sound sleep. I looked across the bedroom and checked the electronic clock.

08:00.

Ugh, I thought, trying to remember what day and month it was.

Saturday?

I reached for the Binatone phone on my bedside table.

'Hello,' I said.

'Andy?'

'Huh?'

I recognised the voice immediately and wondered why she might be phoning so early on a Saturday morning. I was about to ask a question – 'Don't you know what time it is?' – when it occurred to me that she might have a good reason.

'We've found him,' she said. Her voice sounded excited.

'You've found him?' I replied. My voice was still thick with sleep.

Found who?

Aha.

Then I came awake quicker than I ever had before.

'It's one of the four adoption certificates we called up,' said Louise Archer. 'I think I have his adoption certificate in front of me. Can we check the details?'

'We certainly can.'

We checked the details.

The date of birth was correct.

The registration district was correct.

The name of the court was correct.

'The adoption certificate has the full names of his parents and their address at the time it went to court,' said Louise.

'And his name?'

'The certificate has his name.'

She told me his name.

My knowledge of his post-adoption name reversed thirty years of powerlessness. What came to me now was a sense of calm. I didn't have to wonder about all the men of the same age now. I had a name. I could concentrate on one person of that name.

I knew his name.

My first thought was to find a way of contacting Carol. I wanted to tell her his name.

Or maybe she knew already.

I was living in a beautiful part of the world at that time. The day I discovered his name was a stunning late-summer day. It was my favourite time of the year. The trees were turning, the sun was shining, and I set off for a three-hour walk. It was quiet and beautiful. I had a spring in my step.

Part of my trek involved a mile-long disused railway line that curved around the side of the valley. I was walking from one end, the track to myself, when I saw a runner coming towards me. She was tall, dark-haired, with a pony-tail that bobbed across her shoulders. She was running superbly. She looked like a top-class middle-distance athlete or one of the local fell runners who wore WOMEN WITH ALTITUDE T-shirts.

I was walking with a sprightly gait, she was running with a loping stride, and we both seemed in great form. We neared each other quickly and she was really stretching her legs. She glided past me with a beaming smile that must have mirrored my own.

It was such a beautiful day and everyone in the world seemed capable of anything.

I phoned my search buddy Nan and told her about my discovery. Nan immediately spotted something very synchronistic about my son's surname.

'That is really freaky,' I said.

Nan was making progress, too, in her search for her half-brother. The death of her grandmother in the United States had opened up a path for her. Florida state law required the next of kin to give permission for cremation, so Nan's name appeared next to her half-brother's full name on the consent form.

She now knew that her half-brother lived in Tokyo, Japan. She had emailed him and spoken to him on the phone. But how and where does someone in Britain meet a relative who lives in Japan?

Louise Archer phoned me back later that weekend to say that she had checked the latest electoral registers.

'His parents are still at the same address,' she told me. 'They've not moved home since the court order thirty years ago…unless it was in the last few months.'

'Why did I not find his date of birth listed on the electoral registers for the year he turned eighteen?'

'I think their address was just outside the catchment area of the library you visited. The court covers one area but the library covered a different area. The electoral registers for his parents' house were kept elsewhere.'

'Or I might have just missed it.'

'I bet you didn't.'

'Probably not.'

'The next stage is to find out where he is living. I can search the electoral registers again and make a list of people of the same name.'

'That would be good. I feel I need some time for all this to settle down. I need some time to revel in knowing his name.'

'Of course.'

'I've also been thinking a lot about Carol.'

'That's understandable.'

'There is so much unresolved between us.'

'Would you like to write something about her?'

'I've started to write about what happened around the time of his birth.'

'That sounds really useful.'

'I'll send it in the next few days.'

'Thank you.'

12

Carol

'This is Carol, dance with each other,' my mate told me. He guided Carol towards me as midnight approached.

Carol and I were teenagers at a fancy-dress ball. My clothes were nothing fancy but she was dressed as a St Trinian's schoolgirl. She wore a white shirt with billowing sleeves, a short black skirt and black tights. Tights were new to Britain. All women's underwear was new to me.

My broken right arm had healed enough for me to hold a pint glass so I had joined my mates in a pub that Friday evening; we'd heard about the hospital dance near closing time. I thought my meeting with Carol was romantic because my parents had first seen each other at a dance in the same town. My Mum was eighteen and my Dad twenty when they met so I had a role model for a meaningful relationship discovered at a relatively young age.

Within the first few minutes Carol and I discovered that our birthdays were only a day apart. I read a lot into such coincidences when I was young. Here was fate, destiny and design – we were obviously meant for each other – but my youthful bravado kept me from admitting that I was hooked.

For our first date Carol and I met in our town's market square. It was a designated meeting point where disparate individuals gathered as the town-hall clock neared its chimes. Everyone in town had heard a story about a boy and girl copping off with each other when their two real dates failed to show.

Carol's father drove her to the market-square. I saw them arrive and watched as they sat and talked for a few moments in the car. Maybe he was checking me out or giving her instructions. I caught a glimpse of him in the car as he sped away.

Carol wore a tweed suit she had made herself. We went for a drink. We talked about what it was like for both of us as only children. We probably talked about other things but mostly we looked at each other. Later we kissed.

In my spare time and school holidays I worked as a forecourt attendant at a petrol station. I went home smelling of petrol and Swarfega and thought I was a real man. I was allowed to borrow second-hand cars that were on sale at the garage. The Austin Mini and Hillman Imp were too small for my lanky frame and a Humber Hawk far too big. I settled on a Hillman Minx.

We were the first generation of teenagers to have access to vehicles. Girls and boys were no longer chaperoned. One night I parked the car in a clearing down a country lane and Carol and I got into the back seat. We had discarded a couple of items of clothing when Carol heard the scratching near the rear window.

'There's someone there,' she said.

'Is there?' I asked.

We dressed quickly and she jumped into the driving seat. We took forever to clear the steamed-up windows. Then she drove up and down the lane, shining the headlights into the verges. We stopped and got out to look at the car. There were hand-marks on the boot, just below the back window.

Carol and I lived only fifteen minutes' walk from each other so our relationship progressed. We saw each other often. But my father lost his job and our family's future became uncertain.

My dad found work 200 miles away and my mother occasionally visited him there. I had the run of the house when they were away and I got to know my girlfriend better. We met several times a week and went to parties and other events together. It was a hedonistic, hormonal time and I was hungry for experience. I didn't want to live life vicariously. I wanted to be involved. I thought about how life could be short and how much I would hate to die without experiencing sexual intercourse. I felt insecure about the future. I suppose that happens when your father loses his job and the family lifestyle is disrupted.

Carol and I took advantage of being alone in my parents' house. My memories of those weeks are vibrant. I began to learn the smells and sounds of sex in beds of cotton sheets and candlewick bedspreads. We managed a few untrained consummations while the coast was clear.

'You could do one of three things,' my father told me, when he returned one day. 'You can do your last year at school here and we can find you some digs. You could leave school now, live in digs and find a job here. Or you could move with us and complete your education up there. Which do you fancy?'

My mother was distressed by the prospect of a move to an outpost 200 miles away and I had mixed feelings. I didn't want to leave my girlfriend or my other friends. But I wanted to be with my parents and I knew that I wouldn't do much schoolwork if I stayed where I was for my last year at school. There would be too many side-attractions, such as parties, sport and fancy-dress dances.

At the time I believed in a natural approach to life: sport without training, food without cooking and exams without revision. My last school report had been condemning. The headmaster had written to my parents to say that he wasn't sure that I'd pass my A levels. He recommended that I leave school and get a job in computing. The only reason for me to stay on at school, according to the headmaster, was his concern that the school's football and cricket fortunes might sag without me. The letter contained a handwritten postscript: *Have just seen him knock up a fine fifty against the staff.*

I moved with my parents even though it meant that Carol and I would be 200 miles apart. Carol and I met three times in the next three months. The conception happened at my parents' house on one of her visits to the north. We had half an hour without supervision before meeting our parents at a town-centre hotel, so we took the opportunity. The point of conception has left an indelible mark on my memory. I can still close my eyes and call up the sight and feel of her body, the ambience of the room and the background and foreground noises at the moment my sperm changed our lives.

After that Carol and I didn't see each other. Months passed. We spoke on the phone once, twice, thrice. She seemed distant in ways other than miles. I thought she had lost interest in me. I thought she'd met someone else. I convinced myself that she'd pulled away from our relationship and moved on with her life. So I let that happen.

Meanwhile, I grew up a little. I learned something about contraception and considered the risks I had been taking. I was lucky to get away with that, I thought. I'll be sensible and restrained in future.

In my new hometown I studied more diligently, missed a fortnight of school with glandular fever and played sport. I got to know the school careers officer and he was very helpful. I looked through the books for a career that had something to do with statistics. He suggested people I could talk to.

Late one Friday afternoon I sat in the local offices of Royal Insurance. The two men across the low table were leaning forward, their hands clasped between their knees. They looked bright, relaxed and enthusiastic.

'So what are you looking for?' one asked.

'I'm looking for a job where I can use my statistics. There's something called an actuary.'

'Actuarial work is a long training,' one man said.

'Can take about seven years,' the other added.

'Oh,' I said.

'There's a lot who fall by the wayside during the training,' the first said. 'They end up as actuarial clerks.'

'We'd advise you to go straight into the insurance side,' the other added.

The only thing that held me back was the precarious nature of my father's job. I expected my parents to move again. So instead of joining my local Royal Insurance office I took a job in Liverpool as a trainee statistical assistant at £750 a year. When I signed a three-year service agreement with Littlewoods Mail Order Stores, Carol was six months pregnant. I didn't know that though. I thought I was heading to Liverpool for an independent life.

I learned about the baby by chance. My parents and I returned from holiday abroad and called in to see old friends in the town where we used to live. I borrowed my parents' car and went to visit Carol. It was 10am one Sunday and the curtains were closed. That was very unusual. It was normally an up-and-at-em, crack-of-dawn household. Maybe there was a death in the family. I knocked on the door and nobody answered.

I went away and then returned an hour later. This time the door was opened. Her parents seemed sombre as they escorted me into the lounge. I felt like I was going into the headmaster's study. I sat down and they told me that Carol had just had a baby.

A wave of shock dropped from the ceiling. It tied my hands behind my back, stuffed cotton-wool into my mouth and pinned my stomach to the chair-seat. The quiet lingered.

'Can I see her?' I asked, at last, when I'd learned how to talk again.

'No, that wouldn't be for the best.'

I could barely string two sentences together. I was shaking inside. It's taught me the value of keeping people informed as events unfold rather than shocking them after the events have happened.

'Boy or girl?' I asked.

'Boy. Do you admit that you're the father?'

'We did have sexual intercourse one time when she visited me.'

Alone in the car, after that meeting with Carol's parents, I tried to contain my hysteria.

'At least it's not twins,' I said aloud, giggling nervously.

I went to visit a mate and shut the birth out of my mind during the hour I was with him. Then I left his house and it all came back.

I drove to the hotel where my parents were having lunch with a dozen others. I arrived late and joined them all for a meal. Afterwards I manipulated my parents into the same car. In the car-park I told them what had happened. They were stunned.

'Your father and I never did that before we were married,' my mother said.

Thanks, Mum, but that's not very helpful, I thought. I already felt that I had let them down. I drove them to Carol's parents.

I have no memory of the five of us together but I know that the meeting took place. There were two couples and me. Two important people were missing – Carol and the baby.

I didn't see Carol.

I never saw, touched or smelled the baby.

As we travelled the 200 miles home my parents and I were generally quiet. Maybe we were all processing what we'd heard. It had been clear at the meeting that the notion of adoption was uppermost in the minds of Carol's parents.

It was a lot for the three of us to digest. When we spoke it was through non sequiturs.

'There's things you can use, Andrew,' my mum said, from the back seat.

'I'm going to stop drinking,' I said. 'Just in case I let something slip out.'

It felt like the birth had to be a secret. It mustn't be revealed to anyone.

I drove the family car for part of the journey. I lost concentration behind the wheel and nearly missed the turn to the services on the A1. The car slewed as I braked too quickly and tried to haul the car through ninety degrees at high speed.

'Careful,' said my dad.

'Oh, Andrew,' said my mum.

The three of us were badly shaken.

I was still my parents' child. The legal age of adulthood was twenty-one and I was well below that mark. I was not allowed to vote in a general election and I was not expected to vote in an adoption election. I submitted to the actions of adults in the adoption bandwagon. Very quickly I took on a set of subliminal messages from Carol's parents, my parents, the system and from deep inside me:

Let us try to recreate our lives exactly as they were before the baby.

I have sinned and will be punished.

Let us pretend that nothing has ever happened.

For God's sake, no-one else should know about this.

Let us never be blackmailed.

Let us pray for forgiveness.

I must not talk to Carol on the phone.

Carol and I should not meet each other.

We must go separately to meet a church social worker.

Then let us forget all about it.

Don't mention it again.

Put it all behind us.

Shush.

My memories of the adoption aftermath are hazy. It was as if I was hypnotised. These days I find that talking to people helps me remember things, but I didn't talk to anyone outside the family about the adoption. I've also found that writing helps me remember, but no notes or records from that period survive. The adoption process taught me to destroy all evidence and I probably wanted to forget about the event.

I was incapable of putting up a fight. I was expected to be like a cuckoo rolling someone else's egg out of the nest with no concern about whether or not it would land safely. The adoption decision was presented to me in such a way that I had to be very strong in order to scupper that decision and find another option. I had a dearth of information and insufficient experience of life. I ruled out surrogate parenting because I knew of no-one who had offered. I ruled out the prospect of Carol and me jointly raising the child because I assumed that she was going along with the adoption and that our relationship was over.

I was reassured by one thing. My father had been adopted and I figured that he'd had a fine life so adoption couldn't be too disastrous. Of course, it was only much later that I discovered how much his adoption had affected him. Only later did I learn about how he was affected by having three brothers with a different surname to his own. Only later did I read that all adopted people suffer some sort of primal wound.

Family life has peculiar ways of being cyclical, replicating a segment of the genogram in another generation. Here I was replicating the role of my father's real father. I didn't know that of course. I didn't have much knowledge about my parents' backgrounds at that time. My parents were risen working-class and adept at papering over cracks. I lived in a culture of verbal boundaries. My parents relayed Carol's parents' instructions to me, stressing that Carol and I must not talk to each other or meet before the adoption was sealed.

It was far too late for abortion to be an option. But a new Abortion Act was soon to change the decision-making options at an early stage of pregnancy. Isn't it strange that abortion and adoption are so different and yet three-quarters of the letters are the same?

A fortnight later I borrowed my father's car and drove 200 miles to see a social worker in the town where I'd first met Carol. I parked the car, found the social worker's office and prepared myself for the interview. Carol's parents had told my parents that I had to be adamant about the adoption and adamant that Carol and I would never get married. I'd had to look up the word *adamant* in my dictionary. It wasn't a word that suited my personality at the time.

The social worker was jolly and friendly. She asked me questions about my school and my A levels. Then she looked for ways to describe me.

'Colour of your eyes?' she said. 'Shall I say brown?'

I shrugged. I was good at shrugging.

'We try to find parents with similar colouring,' she continued. 'Your hair is fair.'

'Fair.'

'What are your hobbies?'

'Sport. I play football, cricket and occasionally rugby.'

'Any other things?'

'Bridge and chess.'

'Oh, chess. That's good.'

I never wanted to play chess again after that.

'Are you willing to sign a consent form?' she asked.

'I suppose so.'

I didn't understand what was happening. It didn't really matter whether I signed a form or not. Carol's signature was all they needed to crank up the adoption process. The family adopting the child had the right to change Christian names and surnames and thereafter the path to my son grew mistier, murkier and muddier. The portcullis had been brought down with me on the wrong side and I'd only just got my feet out of the way in time.

Carol and I were briefed to tell the adoption agency that we would never marry each other. Forms were signed.

I will never marry her, I said.

I will never marry him, she said.

Reader, I married her.

13

Autumn 1998

I travelled long-distance to meet the social worker who oversaw my son's file. While in the Social Services waiting area I thought more about my life and the impact of knowing his name. I had moved to the Peak District to create the time in my life to manage my search. I had embraced the void. And now a name had come into the space I'd created.

I had no job, no woman, no car, no house, no pets and very few possessions. I seemed to be staying clear of a full-on relationship until I had resolved my pattern of relationship catastrophe. I sensed that knowledge of my son was critical to understanding myself.

I was called through to meet the social worker.

'Is it all right for a student to sit in with us?' the social worker asked me.

'Yes, of course,' I said.

I sat down with the two women. They could have been mother and daughter, but the mother figure was hardened to the ways of the world and the daughter was fresh-faced with a natural smile.

Only later did I realise that it wasn't all right for the student to sit in. I should have said 'No'.

'I can confirm that nobody has tried to trace,' the social worker said.

Except me, I thought.

'What are your goals in doing this?' the social worker asked.

It was a fair question. I reeled off what I had written earlier for

Louise.

'Can you take rejection?' the social worker asked.

'Yes, of course,' I said. 'I have thought that through. I have to take that possibility. I know that. My main aim is to make it easy for him to contact me if he so wishes.'

Rejection? I had felt rejected for thirty years, rejected by a system that didn't involve me in the decision. I didn't say that though. There was a young, open-faced student in the room.

The social worker told me that I couldn't see the file yet as some of the information relating to me also applied to the birth mother.

'My next step is to try to contact the birth mother,' I said. 'I have an intermediary and would go through her.'

'We'd advise you not to use anybody outside us and NORCAP,' the social worker said.

That was the point at which she lost my trust. Maybe I'd brought thirty years of mistrust to the table. I had also been pushed away by one set of Social Services for eighteen months before they found the note in their minute-book – *case transferred out of the county*. Maybe my anger had been building up for years.

'My plan is to use the independent intermediary,' I said. 'I'll wait until the birth mother is ready and then approach him directly through the intermediary. But obviously I will take the birth mother's view into account.'

'We'd advise you to approach him through the adoptive parents. We'd need to look at whether the adoptive parents are still alive first.'

I didn't reply. I was suddenly furious.

Go through his adoptive parents?

He was thirty years old and I hoped that he was capable of making his own decisions. I hoped that the adoption juggernaut hadn't made him dependent on his adoptive parents for life. What if Social Services wrote to his adoptive parents and they were against any contact? What if he doesn't speak to them any more?

I can't remember much else of what was said. I remember only my mood. I left with thinly disguised rage. Yes, there were times when a scary anger rose to the surface.

I did one other thing on my trip to see the social worker. I travelled to the town local to my son's parents' address. I looked up copies of the local newspaper for the date that my son turned twenty-one, just to see if there was an announcement in the birthday section. There wasn't.

I looked at the electoral registers and found that he was registered to vote at his parents' house from eighteen to twenty-three.

By now I was adept at finding out where electoral registers and local newspapers were kept around the country. My notebooks were full of addresses and opening hours for libraries and public record offices. No two libraries had the same opening hours or closing days. One was even open on a Sunday.

On the journey back, I stared out of bus windows and train windows, watching people, wondering if they all knew who they were. I regretted the presence of the student at my meeting with the social worker and wished I'd been more assertive about it. I felt as though the student's presence had stopped me from speaking my mind. Just as the system had thirty years before.

Thirty years ago it had needed someone with a strong presence to prevent the adoption. Could I have been strong at that age, in that culture, under that system? I intended to be stronger this time around.

I wrote spontaneous prose in my notebook: *I like the idea of keeping the adoptive parents informed (if they are still alive) but through my intermediary or some other route. Is the social worker's worry to do with my aims? Maybe I'm wanting to stake too big a claim? Or is it my anger and what might spark it? That interview at the time of his birth, my meeting with the [church] social worker, was one of the most devious interviews I have ever given. I was told to take a particular attitude. Sitting with a social worker reminds me too much of the original incident and the insincerity of it. I think what felt wrong was that the system reminded me too much of the loss rather than the resolution. I'm worried that my anger might come out.*

This first meeting with the social worker had been cocooned in distrust. I couldn't believe that she'd wanted to approach the adoptive parents first (and treat the man as a child). The only advantage I could see in this was if my son was unable to read or write, or had other physical or learning difficulties. I could see one major problem in going through the adoptive parents: What if they didn't pass on the letter and wrote back to say that he wasn't interested? (Indeed I later learned of cases where the adoptive parents had not passed on letters. I also saw some figures suggesting that maybe three per cent of adopted people didn't know that they were adopted, and 90 per cent of adoptees approached by birth parents were pleased to hear from them.)

I felt that I had been the victim of a power trip. It was like Social Services were saying, 'We've got the information, you haven't.' In the meeting I'd felt like a teenager all over again.

I was by now firmly convinced that matters were best handled outside the system. I wrote a list of reasons for not using Social Services as an intermediary. I was suspicious of them and thought they might withhold information from me. I had developed a rapport with Louise Archer, who was far more available than Social Services. Louise's big news had come at 8am on a Saturday morning.

The only advantage to using Social Services was that they held the file. But I didn't know what was in that file. It was possible that I already knew all the data in the file.

I challenged my motives again: Was I creating this space in my life so that a child would come into it? I didn't think so. My notebook shows that I was respecting his independence: *Wise up. He's thirty. At that age I acted as if I had no parents. What's the most likely age when he begins to search? A man's thirties is the time for family focus. Will he wait until his parents die? I hope they don't treat him like a child. I would hate anyone having gone to my parents about something important when I was thirty. I should fight against that image of the helpless child.*

Yes, at times during this search I was very angry. At times I ranted. At times I wanted to yell that adoption was a bad thing, that the adoption system was a powerful, well-oiled machine that abused young people. The standard view is that adoptive parents must love their children more because they really wanted them. Nobody dare say anything about how those couples might have been desperate for a child.

In a ranting mood I imagined adoptive parents as infertile couples who never had sex. Then they were awarded the children of highly sexed naughty youngsters, and the children were registered under an alias. Often secrecy prevailed. Surely openness and honesty are best.

During one rant I wondered how Jesse and Frank James might have reacted had they been split up. They wouldn't have stood for it. Then I paused. Considering what they got up to, maybe they should have been separated.

'You don't have to use Social Services at the contact stage, unless you want to,' Louise said. 'I'm still happy to do it.'

It was the day after my meeting with the social worker. Louise had suggested a debriefing meeting in a quiet café in Derbyshire.

'Social Services have the file,' I said.

'It would be useful for you to see the relevant bits of the file at some point, but you don't have to involve them with any of the peripheral stuff.'

'Well, I gave them the chance.'

'Social Services these days are much more professional than the adoption agencies of the 1960s. In the old days the do-gooders had their own agenda. They were amateurs, charity workers, nothing more than middle-class governesses who felt they knew best for the child. They'd have no training, no mentoring, nothing very much. Since then social work has become a real profession. Social workers are trained to recognise abuse, trained to go to court, and so on. Modern-day social workers are up to their eyeballs in difficult work. Would you go looking for records in a dusty basement if you had to appear in court in half an hour? Nowadays children don't get removed unless they are abused or their natural parents are neglectful.'

'I guess I was reliving my meeting with the old-school church social worker.'

'You can't put the 1960s Social Services on a pedestal because they were fallible.'

'What sort of mistakes did they make in adoption issues?'

'They sometimes made blunders in recruiting adoptive parents. Some adoptive parents were dysfunctional. Some divorced later. Mind you, to be fair to adoptive parents, a lot of them have been very good, and some of them weren't told everything about the children they adopted.'

'Do you mean that some children had problems?' I said.

'Yes. Big problems.' Louise waited a moment as if she was debating whether to tell me more. Then she changed tack. 'You need to get to the right person in Social Services. They need pushing. You have to be more assertive towards them.'

Assertiveness wasn't in my nature and it wasn't in my nurture.

'I've heard about adoptive parents who sent a donation every year to the agency,' Louise continued. 'One agency had offices in Knightsbridge. Knightsbridge! Where was that money coming from?'

'How did you find that out?' I asked her.

'A social worker let it slip. The adoptive parents would send a photograph every year with the donation.'

I sensed that Louise was angry on my behalf. At that moment she felt more like my friend than a counsellor, intermediary, detective or philosopher. Today she was wearing conservative clothes and black boots for the colder autumn weather.

'Adoptive parents were sometimes older, more staid, old-fashioned, more right-wing than the birth parents,' Louise said. 'Usually they'd had no children of their own, but sometimes, after adopting, they did conceive. I sometimes wonder what issues a newborn child brought up.'

'Do the adoptive parents all think they are rescuing the children they adopt, by taking them into a comfortable, responsible, stable household?' I asked.

'It may be that some of them subconsciously feel like they are rescuing the child.'

'Might the adoptive parents not have had sex for years, or never had it?'

'I'm not sure that question would have been asked when recruiting adoptive parents thirty years ago,' Louise said.

'Probably not,' I said.

'If a relationship between the adopted child and the adoptive parents breaks up because a birth parent comes on the scene,' Louise continued, 'it's because it was never much of a relationship in the first place. The evidence shows that if an adoption is successful then it doesn't change the relationship with the adoptive parents. The adoptive parents hold different pieces to birth parents. But most birth parents like the pieces they hold. They much prefer to hold those pieces.'

'I hope I'll get there.'

'You will. Keep going.'

'I will.'

Louise paused for some time.

'You look thoughtful,' I said.

'Yes, I was thinking,' said Louise. 'Adopted people often say that their parents have told them that they were special because they were chosen. But actually it's the other way round. It's the adoptive parents who've been chosen for the child. And being chosen is not a totally secure place to be; if you're chosen you can also be unchosen. Some people prefer to say that it's the adoptive parents who were chosen so that it puts the emphasis on the parents to shape up rather than the adoptee.'

'I've got to accept that I was projecting my anger on to the social worker.'

'On the other hand the social worker you've just seen might have been shocked because it was the birth father searching. It's rare for a birth father to do the tracing.'

'I hadn't thought of that. She might have been surprised rather than protective.'

'She might have been protective too.'

'Dealing with a man rather than a woman.'

'It's not what they're used to in the job,' Louise said. 'They think birth fathers can detach themselves more easily.'

'Or birth fathers get detached from the system more easily. Some of them probably don't even know that they are birth fathers.'

Many of us birth fathers are depicted by an empty space on a birth certificate, I thought. But we should never deduce anything from an empty space: it doesn't mean that the birth father is unknown to the birth mother; it doesn't imply the father was totally absent or uncaring; and you certainly cannot conclude that the father does not wish to meet and know his offspring.

'Talk to Social Services,' Louise said. 'If people don't tell Social Services how difficult it is, they won't learn anything. Write to Social Services. Tell them you think they are doing it wrong, and these are the reasons why they are doing it wrong. I bet a lot of these agencies don't even have a policy for dealing with birth fathers.'

'I wish I had an ordinary family,' I said.

'There's no such thing as an ordinary family,' she said, laughing.

'True. And there's no such thing as a straightforward person in authority.'

'So young and yet so cynical,' Louise said.

'Do you think being a birth parent has shaped my attitudes to authority?'

'I don't know. Has it?'

'I don't know either.'

'Try writing about it. See what comes up for you.'

'Good idea.'

We looked out across the gardens that were being

reconstructed.

'This town is on the up,' Louise said. 'Is there any work for people?'

'A friend of mine said recently that the two main industries in town are tea-shops and charity outlets.'

'I keep seeing adverts for Full Monty or Chippendales tribute acts around here.'

'That's the new masculinity,' I said.

Louise nodded.

'It's cold up in these hills,' she said.

'They don't do the Full Monty outside. It's usually in a hall or a club.'

'Ho ho.'

'I think the adoption was a fait accompli,' I said. 'I think that was the reason why I was angry with the social worker. She was a symbol of how I was treated at the time. Much as I can analyse and say that the adoption was all done and dusted before I got there, part of me still thinks I should have been more assertive.'

'I think it was very hard to fight against it in the 1960s unless you threw a histrionic episode,' Louise said.

'I was still a dependant.'

'You just couldn't see yourself in the role of a father at that particular time. You had your head set on other goals and this was not part of the plan. And then these people came along and resolved your problem by taking it out of your hands.'

'A church agency,' I added.

'These days it is normal for social workers to have a student with them. That's part of belonging to a real profession. But it created another triangle for you. You felt overpowered like you had originally. Maybe the social-work student symbolised Carol's inability to fight at the time. I don't know. It was just that there was something about the situation that set you off.'

'I shouldn't have got so angry.'

'There's a lot of anger swilling around adoption. There's nothing wrong with you; it was just that a sperm escaped. You can direct your anger at that sperm if you wish.'

No, I thought, I won't pick a fight with that sperm. Or at least I'll wait to see how that sperm turned out.

I thanked Louise and we said goodbye. Then I sat and thought for a while longer. My resolve had returned. I needed this conversation as an antidote from the meeting with the social worker and her student. There was a lot to take in. It was true that good relationships could overcome every discovery. I had accepted flawed personal histories from people in the past, especially women, and the adoptive parents should be able to accept everything about their adopted son's past. But was there some basic insecurity in the adopted parents? Did they really feel that their child was only on loan?

14

Attitudes to authority

At university, while my son grew from four to seven, I was a person who respected authority. I'd had good relationships with my bosses at work and understood that hierarchies were inevitable. As a mature student I gravitated towards responsible positions. As president of my hall of residence, I sat on university committees and liaised over rent strikes. As treasurer of the Athletic Union I was responsible for a substantial budget, and I edited the Athletic Union Handbook. Fatherhood had emerged in me – I was often the one taking charge – but my fatherhood was diverted into sideroads of other responsibility. But gradually I began to distance myself from the complex structure of institutions and authority. Part of me wanted to be independent and outside the system. I wrote about it in my university notebook:

There is this desire of mine to become detached, stemmed out of learning logic and related to the emotional upsets, continued in the football refereeing, the statistics, the empirical side of sociology. I believe now that it is not a natural characteristic to be detached, more a necessary feature if I want to learn the best way to be attached. Sooner or later I'm going to mellow (another word for growing up?) and want to settle. But do I want children?

I liked university life. I liked not being part of the institution of marriage. I loved my fresh start. I enjoyed other students' assumptions that I'd had no life before university. And I liked the university setting because there were no young children around.

My gradual detachment could have resulted from my upbringing as an only child. Or it could have been because I was older than most students at university. Or it could have been because I had been thrown adrift from the system by the adoption authorities and was busy healing from that one incident. After the adoption nobody in authority sat me down and said, 'This is a very significant life event, one that will haunt you from hereon, let us know what you would really like to do.' I resented that. I began to resent authority.

In my positions of authority at university I began to see how hard it was to satisfy a few hundred people, even when I conducted opinion surveys. I saw how the world was full of watered-down theories, carte-blanche managerial decisions and satisfying the majority at the expense of creative thinkers and outsiders. I was also slowly developing a dislike of ceremony. As an emerging individual I was never going to be able to follow a political creed. I could sense my voice disappearing. I grew to dislike hearing people in power making black-and-white statements.

After doing an MSc degree in Canada I worked as a marketing statistician for a company based in Nottingham. I earned over £4,500 a year and could have saved enough to buy a terraced house outright. But the work no longer suited my ethos. Part of me was losing interest in statistical analysis of the mass market. I was happy to have a detached and objective role but I wanted to study small groups in detail rather than millions of people superficially. Most of the company's workers seemed to feel a responsibility only to their family and the company, whereas I felt responsible for our 17.5 million UK customers. I knew I couldn't satisfy that brief.

I was also aware of how singular I had become. How many other men had grown up as the only child of a football-club manager, fathered an adopted child, studied sociology and statistics as a mature student, lived in Ontario (Canada) and Kentucky (USA) and written a Master of Science thesis on the sociology of sport? I had to accept that I was an individual responsible for myself. *You are the best qualified person to manage your career and you know it,*

I wrote in my notebook.

Thereafter my life as an employee was occasionally fractious. On the surface others saw me as a good worker, getting on with the business, relatively uncomplaining, well liked, well disciplined, but my resentment festered. In Canada I hit back angrily with a survey of past students to suggest improvements to the course. After finishing my job as a milkman I successfully took my employer to court because they had failed to pay me contracted bonuses. I fell out with two other employers for no great reason except that something was unresolved in my life. When I left my Student Services job I was angry because they had taken so long to renew my full-time contract and my colleagues had been earning 50 per cent more than me. I could be the classic barrack-room lawyer at times.

Often, when I left a job, I was grumpy about something because I distrusted the system. Usually it was the hidden authority that I begrudged. I could be angry at any sign of the sort of unfairness that had dogged the adoption process. I hated the party-line because it had let me down. It may have been easier for me to handle work injustices if I'd had a family to serve. Maybe when a man has an integrated home life as ballast he can go home to forget about work and enjoy his children, but I had no good reason to put up with it.

I was working as a milkman in Cambridge when I met Elaine. My son was nine at the time. As a developing outsider who distrusted authority I could identify with other singular people. Elaine was outrageous, ebullient and incorrigible, but she settled with me off and on for over four years. We lived together for half that time.

Elaine was also a feminist. My guilt about Carol's baby had left me with a debt to pay to women. One way I could express this was by supporting feminists who felt betrayed by the system. Maybe some feminists were attracted to me because I seemed to understand that people in authority dealt marked cards. I felt marginalised by politicians, employers and the adoption process.

My life with Elaine took me to all parts of Cambridge. In between delivering milk to the working-class Arbury estate and council houses off Newmarket Road I heard Ann Oakley talk about the sociology of housework and listened to Tony Giddens lecture without notes about the complexities of class, capitalism, conflict and competition. I also enjoyed Cambridge's intellectual graffiti:

THE QUEEN RULES UK
SLIDE RULES 0.1K
SYNONYMS GOVERN ALL RIGHT
LEGALISE CANNABIS…CANNIBALISE LEAVIS

Elaine was twenty-seven and I was approaching thirty when we met. She wanted equal rights for women but she also wanted a child. In our time together she helped me delve more deeply into my motivations for not wanting children. My anti-children argument made some rational sense but I ignored positive reasons for having children, and my real reason for not wanting children was that my first experience of fatherhood had been unrewarding and traumatic. It took me years to face up to the barriers constructed by that first experience. Not until I was with Elaine did I confront my previous trauma. Part of me had always sensed that I was not the right person for a woman who wanted children but I didn't fully understand why I was not right.

Elaine helped me face up to the parenting issue because it was on her agenda. My first experience of having a child was a negative one, and having another child would force me to relive that negative experience. The period after a birth is when a mother needs utter support. What she least needs is to have her man wrestling with an incident in his past. Elaine grew impatient with me.

'I know you are going to get somewhere eventually,' she told me, 'but I need to get there more quickly.'

'We live in difficult times,' I said. 'I need to be more secure.'

It was the early days of Thatcherism. The country had been

saved from inflation at the expense of unemployment.

'You can't think things through when it comes to children,' she said. 'You've just got to get on with it. It's an emotional decision.'

'I need to be in a better position financially to raise children.'

'Kids don't cost that much. They eat beans on toast. Parents don't spend as much money on other things once they've got children. They stay in more.'

I didn't spend much money on anything. But I was a far more complicated person than my argument. I feared being trapped in a job, trapped in a relationship, trapped in my whole life. My first attempt at mating, working and 'parenting' had been so unhappy.

Elaine and I split up after eighteen months together. She had been unhappy about aspects of our relationship from the start.

'I want to be out doing things,' she told me. 'I want to be engaged in life.'

'Yeah, I'm just an observer,' I said.

'I don't like my selfishness but it's been magnified by your unselfishness,' Elaine told me.

'These are things I have to do at the moment,' I said. I was thinking about the book I was working on. Writing was another form of detachment from authority that suited me.

'You come across as someone who will eventually go a long way,' Elaine told me. 'But you're taking your time, slowly thinking through each stage, making sure everything is right. It drives me crazy.'

I thought about my reply for a long time.

'You set high standards for yourself,' Elaine continued, 'and therefore constantly prove yourself as a failure.'

I nodded.

'Be easier on yourself,' she said.

I was still thinking.

Elaine had her eye on another relationship. She wanted me to move out and wanted it to happen immediately. I thought she was being unkind as it threw my life into chaos overnight. But that was just her personality. She was spontaneous and impulsive. I had to learn more of that.

Elaine and I got back together again a few months later. This time we weren't living with each other, but we got on well. She was twenty-nine, going on thirty, and even more interested in having children.

After another year together, though, she grew frustrated with me again. I wasn't living my life emotionally enough. I tended to be a statistician and a sociologist. She would read something in the newspaper and react angrily or joyously but I would analyse it to death.

'Five times as many violent crimes and four times as many property crimes are committed than reported to the police,' I told her one day. 'Only one out of two burglaries are reported and only thirteen per cent of vandalism acts.'

I was similarly appalled at the under-reporting of car-crash deaths in national newspapers. Car-crash deaths only seemed to be reported if there was a multiple pile-up, more than one death occurred, a celebrity was involved or there was something quirky about the event. Yet all aeroplane deaths were reported. Most people ended up being scared of flying and confident about road travel. I was the other way round.

All this rationality of mine was useless when a friend of Elaine's was killed in a car crash. What she needed from me was an emotional response. She wanted me to say, 'Let's get married and have a child.' On the surface Elaine seemed vehemently opposed to marriage but when we broke up for the second time she explained that her criticism of marriage was pure jealousy.

Elaine married a year later. She married a man who knew that he wanted children. When it came to marriage and children for me, however, my stance was always 'Wait'. My financial side was still not secure but I wondered which came first. Maybe I never allowed myself to be financially strong so that I couldn't take that step towards parenthood. Maybe my first experience had put me off for life.

A party in Cambridge. The hosts were two sociologists. The conversation was thoughtful, engaging and polysyllabic. Despite my sociology background I felt a little overawed whereas Elaine enjoyed the party atmosphere and said what she thought.

At the corner of one room I found a similar wallflower to myself. She was in her early thirties with ginger hair and a pale complexion. She was very shy and blushed easily. She told me that she was separated from her husband and was bringing up a child on her own. She lived for her child. She was unaccustomed to parties like this.

'Do you have children?' she asked me.

'No,' I said.

She looked away from me and stared across the party scene.

'When you've brought a child into the world,' she said, 'You really feel that you have achieved something.'

I nodded without knowing why.

From the age of thirty I increasingly felt like a society outsider. I became a multi-part-timer with a smorgasbord of work. One of my numerous transient jobs was as an outdoor clerk on a big Thames Valley Police sexual abuse case. I learned a lot about sexual abuse from talking to expert witnesses and barristers during the case. In the next decade I read lots of claims of sexual abuse against people in positions of religious authority. I learned to distrust the type of religious authority that had streamlined the adoption of my son.

The adoption slowly turned me off organised religion for life. A church agency failed to take my feelings into account. A church agency failed to offer help or counselling. A church agency kept Carol and me estranged from each other after our child's birth. A church agency failed to point out that there were ways that we could have kept the baby. A church agency didn't believe that we had the freedom to choose what to do with our baby.

Maybe some people turn towards religion after such events. I can understand that. I've known some very religious people with a seemingly shameful event in their past – the sexologist John Money has said that if you show him self-righteousness he will search for the sin – but I didn't turn to religion. Instead I became suspicious of religious organisations. At university I learned that religion was a sociological function of society. Religion was there to provide support, consolation, reconciliation, security, identity and solidarity. It was there to provide solace against imminent death, a set of values and sacred norms, a guide to what was right or wrong. Sadly, it was in this last arena that I lost faith. When it came to adoption initiatives in the 1960s and 1970s I did not believe that religious fanatics had done the right thing.

15

Winter 1998–99

On New Year's Eve I went to bed before midnight and woke up in the early hours of 1999. A dream was fresh in my mind and I wrote it down. I was sitting in the back row of a huge amphitheatre watching a play. I could see Carol's parents far below me as they sat in the front row. Then I saw Carol with her husband in another row below me. In my dream Carol had long hair, greying, tied and bunched. We were all watching the drama, all on the edge of our seats, all straining to see how the play ended.

On a trip to Scotland my train approached the town where Carol and I had conceived our son. After leaving school I could have easily stayed in this town had I accepted the job at Royal Insurance. What if Carol and I had taken on the baby, she had joined me in the north and I had stayed in insurance for thirty years?

Would we have stayed together in this alternative life?

Possibly. I was loyal and believed in fate at that time.

I thought about this for a few miles as the train approached the rail station and I saw symbols of my previous life. I even saw buildings that had played a part on the night of conception. On the train I could easily have let the tears flow freely as I thought about the life I had missed, but it would not have been very British to sob spontaneously among strangers. I trapped a mugful of tears behind the skin of my face and left them there.

The train was leaving the station now. My mind left the town and returned to my real life. I knew that I really liked my life as it had actually turned out. Occasionally it had been a painful, troubled journey but it had also given me a very different perspective on the world. I had achieved things I would never have done in my other life. The trauma had helped to open me up. I had shared powerful conversations about important life events. I could tune into others of the same ilk. My life had brought me many intimate rewards and some wonderful friendships. I'd had exciting relationships and had found my place outside the system. As a writer without a regular muse or a secretary or an agent I'd developed an I-did-it-on-my-own confidence. I trusted my independence. It was a dream world of sorts. I was the only one who knew how hard it had been at times.

I travelled to Scotland to meet my search buddy Nan. We caught up with our relevant family stories. Nan hadn't given up hope of meeting her half-brother in Japan and I still hoped for a meeting with my son. My visit to Nan coincided with the arrival of her mother's cousin from the United States. The four of us wrote out Nan's family tree on the back of a roll of wallpaper.

I read the letter Louise had drafted and then handed it back.

'Perfect,' I said. 'The key point is discreetly made.'

I am writing about a confidential matter that happened thirty years ago.

'I'll mark the envelope Private and Confidential,' Louise said.

'And you think the time is good? Christmas is far enough in the past?'

'Yes, I think so.'

It was nearly six months since I'd discovered my son's name but there had been little tangible movement forward. It had taken me a while to recover from the episode with the social worker. Now I felt that Carol deserved an opportunity to start dealing with the issue. Whatever her circumstances I felt that it was courtesy to keep her informed. I knew it could cause problems for her but I felt I had to do it. I'd reached the stage where I couldn't pass a can of worms without getting out my can-opener.

Louise Archer's search for Carol had proved much easier than the one for my son. We knew Carol's maiden name in full and we soon confirmed her married name. Then we were fairly sure that we knew her address.

'What if my son is in the process of trying to contact his birth mother, or if she is making enquiries of her own?' I asked Louise.

'Well, it is probably better to contact Carol and see if that is happening. If she doesn't wish any contact, how will that affect you?'

'I don't think it will affect me. I'll carry on anyway.'

'What if she insists that you don't do this?'

I had to think about that one. We were in Louise's house so I looked at the blackboard on her wall. It was as though I was trying to read what had been written during the last lesson.

'That's different,' I said. 'I'd have to think carefully about that. I suppose it would depend on her reasons for not going on. I might stop if they are good enough reasons.'

'What if he's contacted her already without going through the file?'

'That's possible. Carol wouldn't know where I was. I'm relatively hard to find now that my parents have gone.'

We talked a little about my name not being on the birth certificate.

'Technically they can't put the father's name on the birth certificate unless the man accepts that he is the father,' Louise reminded me. 'The husband's name would automatically go on the certificate if she was married. If she wasn't married the only way to get the father's name on the certificate was for the father to be present when the birth was being registered. If you'd been allowed to put anybody down as the father you'd have lots of bogus Mick Jaggers and John Lennons.'

'Would she have had to go to the registry office?'

'No. She could have registered the birth in the hospital. And she might not remember doing that. She was probably in shock at the time. She would be in the hospital, alone and traumatised, knowing that the baby was going to be adopted. It could have been a real mental and psychological torture. You can be very submissive in that situation. They'd keep the two parties – the mother and father – apart from each other.'

'Like the interrogation of criminals,' I said.

'She'd probably be with the baby until they came out of the hospital, unless she discharged herself beforehand. She'd then have the chance to go to see the foster parents about six weeks later. Some women didn't go. Some found it too hard to do that. Going to the foster parents was a very difficult situation. You didn't know whether you had the rights to claim the baby. You didn't know your rights.'

I thanked Louise. We said goodbye and I went away to wait for Carol's response to Louise's letter. In the meantime I read more about adoption issues. In particular I looked at the birth mother's stories. Well, there was virtually nothing about birth fathers.

16

Birth mothers

One classic writing-therapy exercise is to construct part of the story from another person's viewpoint. In my case this meant taking the birth mother's viewpoint and writing the story from her angle. I had talked to a few birth mothers and read many tear-jerking accounts. I eventually constructed a composite account of a birth mother's experience of giving birth when knowing the child will be adopted. So imagine that you are pregnant and likely to lose your child. Sit in a chair or lie down. Take the extra weight off your feet...

For months you may not talk to friends and family about your pregnancy and you hide it from everyone. You may think you've had a period when you haven't really. You may try to hide your bump by wearing baggy clothes, staying in the house or calling in sick. You feel the shame you have brought on your parents by not being married. You may feel even more shame for getting pregnant by a married man. You have no idea how you will cope. You cannot find a way to tell the baby's father that you are pregnant because you cannot deal with another person's emotions as well as your own. You may collapse at work, at school, at college or in the house.

You are hopeful of keeping the child but your parents say 'No' or 'What would the neighbours think?' You may keep the pregnancy so much to yourself that you ignore other people. Or you share your secret only for your confidante to divulge it to someone else. Then you are even more ashamed and upset. You may continue with your life exactly as it was. You may go around in a dream, a state of shock, waiting to wake up as you were before you were pregnant. Or you may register every detail, such as the first time you feel your baby kick, the first time you are sick, or the glow of being pregnant. During your pregnancy nobody seems to listen to you except your child. During your pregnancy you wonder if this may be the only time your child ever feels safe. And, naturally, you are subject to all the side-effects that pregnancy brings.

Someone else in your family may also be pregnant and openly excited about it because she is married. During your pregnancy you go without ante-natal care so you develop complications. You haven't done any breathing exercises. You haven't been supported. The nurses are unsympathetic ('We waited until we were married'). You may feel that you are treated more harshly than other mothers-to-be. Your mother may say, 'How can you do this to us?' A male friend may ask you to marry him even though it is not his child. You may eat heavily in an attempt to look fat rather than pregnant.

You may be sent to a special home or to a relative in a faraway town, as if your condition was contagious. If you go to a mother-and-baby home you might have to work like a slave until you go into labour. You may have to report to a 'moral welfare officer'. You have to be indoors by six, in bed by ten, and are allowed no visitors. You may be given a Woolworth wedding-ring, told to call yourself 'Mrs' and sent to work in a factory in order to pay for your keep in the home. You may be told to keep out of sight and 'keep mum' (an unfortunate expression). You may be marched to church in a crocodile on Sundays.

The actual birth may have complications, such as toxaemia (toxic poisoning) or haemorrhaging, and you are offered little pain relief. You may feel the nurses are enjoying your pain. Your body feels sore and your soul even more so. Someone may suggest that you raise the child as your brother or sister. But ultimately you are faced with a choice that isn't really a choice – adoption or adoption?

You give birth and your body changes in ways that will remind you daily. You gain a stretch mark, a small scar or a different pattern of urinating. No-one says 'Congratulations' or 'Well done'. You give birth and immediately bond with your child. Then you have to unbond with your child and of course that is impossible. Your child may be immediately taken away from you so you are not allowed to hold her, feed her or see her. You may be told not to look at your child. A nurse hands individual babies to the mothers, one by one, until it gets to you ('Not that one, it's being adopted'). You may overhear part of a judgmental conversation ('Someone who gives up their child obviously doesn't care about their child'). You may be lambasted to your face ('You girls get what you deserve'). The nurses may mock your name when calling you 'Miss' while they call the other mothers 'Mrs'. You may have your breasts bound to stop your milk from coming. Or you may breastfeed and mother your baby until your time together is cruelly curtailed.

You have very mixed feelings about registering the birth of your child and naming your child. You may or may not have discussed your child's name with the father. You may not have thought about a name at all. Maybe a nurse gives you a book of baby's names and you pick the first one you see. Maybe the nurse talks you out of other Christian names ('Not much point giving her a second name if she's going and the names will be changed'). You don't know whether to choose a name you like or dislike ('Don't choose a name you like, love, you won't be able to use it again'). You may wonder if it is wise to name your boy child after his father. You may ask for ideas about names from the woman in the next bed. If you leave the hospital with your child you may hide the baby under a coat or a blanket just in case anyone sees you and discovers your secret. You may take special care to conceal your bundle when you pass a bus or the house of someone you know. After a week you hand over your baby to a complete stranger. Your child is suddenly lifted away from you and taken on a journey, like a baby in a basket carried by a stork.

You think about the child's father. Most likely you were in a stable relationship with him. But maybe he was a one-night stand or a married man. You may want the father to see his child. This should be the critical time when you get together as a family – parents and baby – and it should be a joyous celebratory time. But it is not. Instead you are told exactly what to do, precisely what to say, and shown where to sign on the form. You may learn later that the birth father wanted to see you and your baby but your parents, the hospital workers and/or the adoption organisation might have proclaimed that it was inappropriate. At the time you thought that the birth father was absent because he didn't care. You may have had your letters to the birth father intercepted. Or the birth father may have done a moonlight flit. You hurt inside and are alone with your pain.

Then into the boxing ring comes a social worker who throws a moral uppercut ('You've no choice really'), a judicial jab ('It's only fair to the child') and a coercive knock-out punch ('If it doesn't go through now it won't go through'). You hear the results of an undemocratic election ('No one else feels the same way you do'). Nobody explains that you could get a flat and enough benefits to raise the child yourself. From the moment you have gone to your doctor, the slick adoption bureaucracy is in place and your motherhood is threatened. You sign the adoption papers without really knowing what you are signing. You don't realise that you can fight the adoption when it comes to court. Deep down you want to let out a primal scream. You are a wounded animal whose offspring has been captured.

You may lose your faith in religion, or you may take solace in religion. You may even quote verse 15 of Isaiah chapter 49: 'Can a woman forget her sucking child, that she should not have compassion on the son of her womb? Yea, they may forget, yet will I not forget thee.' Or you may see the birth of Jesus as just another adoption story that explains a virgin birth.

After the adoption you might have been told, 'Forget about it now, you've had your punishment, make a fresh start.' Then everyone around you conspires to put your story into a locked box and throw away the key, and you are told, 'It's all in the past'.

But if you get pregnant again, you will have to answer the doctor's question: 'Is this your first child?'

When you walk down the street in the weeks after the adoption it may feel like you are hearing imaginary voices shouting 'Shameful hussy', 'Look at that tart', and 'They should put them in stocks'. But you have kept your secret and returned to your life without anyone noticing what you have been through. You have achieved what Suzanne Arms has called an 'immaculate deception'. But you may worry that no man will want to marry you once he knows that you've had a child. Maybe you erupt in anger and scream at your mother ('It's all your fault') or try to put a spell on the adoptive mother ('That barren bitch has got my baby').

Later in your life, you can start to cry for no reason that's connected to the present. Later in life you can look back at your teenage days and see yourself as young and hopeless with no control over the pivotal incident in your life. The relinquishment of your child was the most stressful event in your life and always will be. You may worry that your birth child's health might be affected because you didn't take especially good care of yourself during your pregnancy. You may worry that you may not be able to bond if you have another baby. You may be concerned about being overprotective if you have another child. You may have deep and lasting grief reactions, bouts of depression, anxiety, alcohol abuse, physical ill-health and a continuing worry about the child's well-being. You find it impossible to shut down the parental feeling. But sometimes you feel a strange calmness as you sense that your child (now an adult) may not be far away.

You think you have dealt with it all, you think you have buried the past, you think you have got on with your life, and then, suddenly, years later, you get a letter saying your birth child wishes contact or that someone in the family has instigated a search. It knocks your life sideways. A brief thought of what you went through so long ago can reduce you to tears. And when there is potential for contact with your grown-up child there are other things you need to consider. You may feel you need to see a solicitor to work out what you are allowed to do and who has a right to your estate. You may have to tell your other children that the birth order is not as it seems and the eldest child is no longer the eldest child or the only child is not really the one and only. Or you may have to tell your husband or boyfriend or girlfriend that you did have a child after all. You mustn't get your expectations too high. You need supportive people around you. You will find that the matter dominates your thoughts.

17

Spring 1999

I was typing conscientiously on my Amstrad 1640 computer, thinking about Jill Dando's death, when the telephone rang. I picked it up on the fourth ring.

'Andy Ward,' I said.

'It's Louise.'

'Good morning.'

'I've just received a letter from Carol.'

'Oh.'

I felt my body shudder slightly.

About seven weeks had passed since Louise had first written to Carol. After receiving no reply in the first six weeks Louise had sent a follow-up letter by recorded delivery. Louise wanted to make sure that Carol was still living at that address.

'Is she OK?' I asked.

'Yes. She says that as soon as she saw Private and Confidential on the envelope she knew that it had to be about her son. She says that her son has always held a special place in her heart but she needs some time to consider every aspect.'

'Aha,' I said. 'I can identify with that.'

'I think I'll respond by saying that I wrote the letter at the bequest of the birth father,' Louise said. 'I'll tell her that we are now at a point where it may be possible for an intermediary to make direct contact with your son on your behalf.'

'Thank you, Louise,' I said. 'Thank you.'

'And thank you for sending me your collage of birth-mother experiences.'

'What did you think?'

'The attitude of the people in authority in those days was astonishing when it came to adoptions. They assumed that mothers could forget that they had given birth to a child. That sounds horrendous now but I think they really believed it at the time.'

Another coincidence. I met a woman at a party. She was married with children of her own. We talked seriously about psychology while people around us danced and joked.

'Do you have any children?' she asked me.

I hesitated, as usual, as if looking at a sign at a crossroads.

'I fathered a child but he was adopted at birth,' I said.

'Are you in touch with him?'

'I'm on a journey to get in touch with him. I think I know where he is. My next stage is contacting Carol and seeing what she thinks about the idea.'

'Whatever you do, don't just turn up on his doorstep.'

'I'm using an intermediary.'

'I wish I'd done that with my real parents. You see, I was adopted. I found out who my real parents were and went round to their house. It was awful. They shut the door on me.'

'Have you tried again through an intermediary?'

'I don't think I could. I feel as though the door's bolted.'

'Too much of a shock.'

'Yes.'

'Andy Ward,' I said when the phone rang.

'Louise Archer. I've had another letter from Carol.'

'Is it good?'

'I think so. She has two questions. She wants to know why you want to find your birth son and she's interested in what we already know about him. She wants to avoid any regrettable action being taken.'

'That sounds good.'

'It's a well-thought-out letter,' Louise said. 'She's asking sensible questions. Perhaps she has good support.'

'Good,' I said. 'Tell her that I want to take her feelings into account before making any approach to him. I don't want it to have an adverse effect on her family. Tell her I want him to know the medical details of our families. And to have him know that he has never been forgotten, etc.'

I ran through my list of six reasons for the search.

'OK,' said Louise. 'Let me check what we know about him.'

By now we had quite a long list of data. We knew my birth son's full adoptive name, his adoptive parents' full names and their current address. We knew he was listed at his adoptive parents' address for five years after reaching the age of eighteen. There was no record of him marrying or dying in England and Wales. We had a long list of current addresses that could fit his current whereabouts. We also knew that he had not asked to see his Social Services file. He had not registered with NORCAP.

'I'll write again with that data and explain where we are with the search,' Louise said.

Carol was quickly brought up to speed. My intermediary rapidly became our intermediary. My detective was now our detective. My Louise was now our Louise. Carol just needed time to adjust to the idea of contact. She needed to see it from all perspectives. She seemed to find it helpful that it was in the open.

I continued to read around my subject. I read and wept through lots of reunion stories. Nothing before or since has made me cry so easily. If I ever need to encourage repressed tears all I have to do is take myself into solitude, dim the lights, read a book such as *Preparing for Reunion* by Julia Feast *et al* and let grief and happiness pervade the room in equal intensity.

While reading *Preparing for Reunion* I noticed that one adopted person referred to her birth parents as 'my proper mother and father'. That gave me yet another label for myself. I was a biological father, birth father, blood father, genetic father, hereditary father, natural father, original father, real father, putative father and proper father.

Carol and I started corresponding directly to each other. There was so much to get through before we could meet, so much more to process before we could contact our son. We had to revisit the story of the birth, review what had happened in our relationship after the birth, and understand our marriage.

18
Marriage

I spent much of the first year of my son's life in a daze. A small patch of psoriasis emerged on my chest. I had difficulties in sleeping and strange visions when I did doze off. I'd had restless nights before – hitchhiking through Europe or in airport lounges – but this time the disturbance came from within me rather than from external interruptions.

A few weeks after the adoption Carol's parents and my parents arranged a secret meeting between Carol and me. While the four parents talked in one of the cars, Carol and I took a short walk into the woods. We were paranoid in case some adoption worker might see us and reprimand us for jeopardising the whole system. It was like being in a seedy television series about blackmail and kidnapping. Carol and I tried to talk but we were hopelessly out of our depth. I can't remember a single thing we said.

Soon after that meeting I went to work in Liverpool. I studied part time at a local college and grew more concerned about my career. In my third week at work I read in the newspaper that my father had lost his job again. I became more sensitive and serious as a person, more separate from my mates, more cautious about what I said to them. As a sportsman I lost some of my competitive edge.

A few months after the birth Carol and I were unknowingly severed from the adoption by court order. The birth and the adoption were both suitably swept under the carpet. The 'bad parents' were out of the picture and the 'good parents' had taken over. My role was to forget it had ever happened. Except that you can never forget something like that, you can only deny it.

My weekends were more likely to be taken up with seeing Carol than playing sport. Either Carol would come to Liverpool or I would take the train to see her. We were drawn back to each other but we also needed the distance. We were very formal together. But we were also trying to find jobs in each other's region of the country. We assumed that we would eventually live in the same town. We got engaged shortly before our son's first birthday.

One day in the second year of his life I was alone at Carol's parents' house when Carol suddenly phoned. She asked me to look through some possessions of hers for something that was needed for our wedding. I found what she needed, but in passing I found something else. What I found was a certificate of confinement with the name of the hospital and the child's date of birth. It was a real shock to see proof of the event. This official form reified the whole thing for me. Yes, it had really happened. I had to admit it. There could be no waking up from a bad dream, no switching off the TV and saying 'It was only a film', no reading in the newspaper that the story had been denied. So far I had managed to detach myself from the event – the adoption decision could have been a question on an examination paper – but now this hospital note sent a wave of emotion through me. My whole philosophy of life was affected as I registered the reality.

I think of that moment whenever I talk to a woman friend who is pregnant and frustrated by her man's nonchalance and unwillingness to engage with the pregnancy. I tell them that the man may take longer to react to the news. The woman is living with the growing event each day. Her body is changing and she is registering those changes. The man must first have a moment when he accepts that the pregnancy is real and that decisions have to be made. Maybe the putative father needs to see a scan, attend a clinic, see an appointment letter or simply be more included.

The adoption left me with fragments of information. Some parts of my constructed story were wrong, some parts right, but most of the story was unknown, waiting to be guessed. Over the years the fragments and guesses became an established code.

I couldn't understand why Carol hadn't told me that she was pregnant. Sometime after the birth I think she told me that she didn't want to interfere with my A-level preparations but I didn't really know.

Having not been kept informed of the pregnancy, it was a great shock when I finally learned about it. But I couldn't really blame Carol for not telling me. She was still a teenager and had no great experience to call on. I was more likely to blame myself, turn my anger inwards, give myself a hard time.

Over the years, I calculated dates many times. I twirled 'forty weeks' and 'nine months' around my mental abacus until I was dizzy. I worked out that the baby was either sixteen days early or I was wrong about the weekend. Or maybe there was someone else; surely, if the parents know there is a steady boyfriend (me) and there is a one-night stand with another, wouldn't it be natural to name the known boyfriend (me) rather than the one-night stand? A man can drive himself mad with this kind of thinking. But the best evidence for me was that it felt like I was the father. Yes, I was reasonably sure.

Carol and I stayed engaged and she found a job as a schoolteacher in a rough area of Merseyside. It was one of those schools where the kids carved their names on teachers rather than desks. It was a very hard adjustment for her and I was of little help. We lived in separate residences five minutes' walk away from each other. Some of this was a charade to appease parents and the public that we imagined was watching. It took some time for any sexual relationship to resume and then it progressed cautiously forward. When Carol was prescribed the oral contraceptive pill we began to revisit the cause of our grief. But I would go home most nights. Staying overnight still felt like a scandal. Our relationship retained the pretence of celibacy.

We progressed in our careers. Carol left teaching and started working in the health service. I assumed more responsibility at Littlewoods Mail Order Stores, working in their new fourteen-story JM Centre. The JM stood for John Moores, the company's founder and chairman. When the staff were given an opportunity to suggest names for the new building, one wag suggested The Old Mooresoleum.

'What do you do at Littlewoods?' people asked me on the rare occasions that I met new people.

'I'm a statistician.'

'What's that when it's at home?'

'I forecast sales and trends, do market research and ad hoc research.'

'Does it need special training?'

'Yeah. You study for three years just to learn how to say the word *statistician*.'

Carol and I were earning well. We borrowed twice our joint salary and bought a three-bedroom house. By the time our birth son passed two we could afford to get married and raise a family.

A few weeks later Carol and I had a big wedding with a hundred guests. She wore white and I spent a week's wages on her 22-carat gold ring and my nine-carat one.

Years later I met up with a friend of mine who had been a guest at the wedding. My friend told me that she had wept during my wedding to Carol, and again during the post-nuptial meal, but her tears were of sadness rather than joy. It was only when I told my friend the story of the baby that her weeping made sense to her. Through that incident she learned that her own emotions could be sensitised to those of other people. Counsellors and therapists learn to trust such sensitivities and work with them.

Carol and I didn't talk about our son but he was always close. Wherever we went we were accompanied by our unanswered wound. The hurt was hidden under newspapers. It was wrapped in the tea-towel we used for drying the dishes. If we went out together the pain came with us in Carol's handbag or my coat pocket. If we took all our clothes off and went to bed together the hurt rose from under the pillows and dropped like a sack of forbidden fruit on to our bodies. It followed us around from room to room, and every time we glimpsed it we hid it somewhere else. Our parents didn't talk about it either. They were suffering their own losses.

Surrogate babies gravitated towards Carol and me. We adopted a stray cat and kept a dog for a while. Hammy the hamster was let out of his cage to run up and down the stairs, and once he climbed into the fireplace and came out covered in soot. We set up a tank of tropical fish. But I felt uncomfortable around pets. Something was still missing.

Would our relationship have worked had it not been for the baby? I find it very difficult to say what my relationship with Carol was like fundamentally. We had been very happy and hungry for each other in the early months, and undoubtedly we had fallen in love. After three years of knowing each other, however, the bulk of our relationship had taken place since the trauma. Joint trauma is always difficult. Often couples grieve in different ways. Sometimes their grieving processes clash and that puts the relationship in jeopardy. I am sure that was the case with us. But maybe there were other differences too. We were both only children but her parents were very different to mine. Her father was very mechanically minded. His main hobbies were fixing the car, fixing the house and fixing the garden, whereas my father was clueless about DIY and believed in 'every man to his trade'. My father spent much less time at home than Carol's father and was more fulfilled in a tracksuit than in overalls.

How do you develop a relationship after such an acute early loss? Does the relationship have anywhere it can go? We tried to move forward but we were haunted by our shared past. We lived together in our own house but our relationship sustained its guilt and confusion. We really needed to confront the trauma but neither of us knew how. Already we were starting to drift away from each other. If our relationship was heading towards having children together, it was heading towards painful memories that were best avoided. Within nine months of married life Carol was leading her own life and I was finding it hard to sleep. I lost weight and was capable of hurting Carol with words if our time in the house overlapped.

We were both very unhappy. I was tired, bored, depressed and isolationist, and Carol wanted to go out in the evenings. On the rare occasions that we met it was hard being around each other. My life seemed to consist of work, part-time education and do-it-yourself-without-help. I felt as though I was a big disappointment to Carol.

I had stopped trusting her after the pregnancy when I probably had no need not to trust her. She was dedicated to me enough to spend months knitting me a complicated sweater (which I still have). It was just that we lacked the articulation to explain our confusion. We were living together but we were living apart.

My parents had moved back to the Midlands. They were renting a flat in an old manor house. The flat had large rooms, high ceilings and inadequate storage heaters. The view from the front windows was of a large lawn and a tethered goat. One day a neighbour was working under his car with loose pages from a car manual laid out beside him. A gust of wind blew away the plans and the goat ate them.

On a cold winter's night, I was sitting chatting to my mother when she gave me a cutting from a magazine. It was a piece of philosophy from Søren Kierkegaard: *to take risks is to risk anxiety, not to take risks is to risk losing oneself.*

It was a deep and material moment, quite out of character for my mother, who had only a basic education, but I appreciated it. Kierkegaard's words changed my life. I had to take risks. I couldn't let my life drift on like this.

A young man on my street was forever working on his house in his spare time. His day job was driving a mole for the new Wallasey Tunnel. We caught the same bus at seven-fifteen in the morning.

'Sometimes I wonder if the hippies have it right,' he told me one day. 'It must beat this daily drudge work.'

'Yeah, I know what you mean,' I said.

I disliked having a job, a wife and a car. I felt trapped. I had given up playing football and cricket, and I hated my current existence. I was stranded on an island full of DIY, car maintenance, study and an 8.30 to 5 job. I wanted a way out. I fantasised about running away. I bought copies of *Farmer's Weekly* and looked at vacancies for agricultural labourers in the north of Scotland.

I lost even more weight. My sleep was disturbed, my confidence drained and I was ashamed of my past. There was an occasion when I scratched the back of my left hand with the nails of my right hand, a few decades before I learned the term self-harm. I thought about suicide. The pain would be over then – the pain of the loss, the pain that was around when Carol and I were together, the pain that was stored in the house. Generally we hid from each other. I was aware that Carol needed me to change in lots of ways but I knew I couldn't change quickly enough. Carol was treated for depression and lack of sleep, and I should have sought help too.

Finally I ran away constructively – I went to university. My way of informing Carol about my decision was to leave my UCCA application form lying around so that she could see it.

I felt I needed an education. I was desperate to understand the world. But there is no way a man can understand the feelings of a woman who carries a baby for nine months and then gives up the child shortly after the birth. No matter how much a man reads, no matter how many experiences he has, no matter how much he studies the literature on bereavement, there is something missing that can only be supplied by experience.

The break-up was uncommunicative and raw. There was a lot of suppressed acrimony. I remember thinking that all it needed was for her to ask me to stay. Having received an unconditional offer of a place at university I spent six months looking for a way to discuss it with her. But I thought she had made it clear that she wanted rid of me, or wanted me to do something that I wasn't capable of doing.

I remember our last brief talk on the day I left.

'What are you going to do after university?' she asked me.

'I don't know,' I said. 'Probably teach.'

'God help the kids,' she said.

For eighteen months or so we had lived different lives, avoiding each other wherever possible. Then we said goodbye with some bitterness and I walked out with two suitcases. Our solicitors drew up a separation agreement and we were divorced four years later. That left me two black marks against my name; I was a divorced man and the father of a child born outside marriage. Carol and I didn't see each other again for twenty-seven years.

19

Summer 1999

Over thirty years after the birth Carol and I needed to negotiate a close relationship that didn't bring back too many painful memories. We both felt responsible for what had happened at the time. We both felt guilty. We had both tried to make it right for our parents. We'd blamed ourselves and each other. And we'd distanced ourselves from each other.

Now I needed to understand all that she went through, and Carol needed to articulate what she felt and how much she regretted what had happened. Over the years I had assumed that I had been very passive over the decision and that she was angry with me for not taking a stance. When we talked thirty years later, however, I found out that she had never been angry with me, just devastated that I'd gone along with the adoption.

It was difficult to know where to start. There was so much that I still felt bad about, mainly because I didn't offer her much support or sympathy at the time of the birth. I was part of the conspiracy to bury the deed and resume normal service. We were both very young and acting well outside our experience.

In our marriage a level of depression was always present after the loss. We both felt we were working around each other's activities, or maybe we had such different interests. We were both hurt and confused. We didn't only lose a baby, we lost each other.

Through our exchange of letters I began to understand a little of Carol's side of the story and I could see how hard it was for her to tell me that she was pregnant. The longer the pregnancy went on, the harder it became. We were not allowed to make an informed choice, not allowed to talk to each other about the situation. Carol wanted me to come into the hospital immediately after the birth but her parents didn't think that was a good idea. To stay in the adoption system we'd had to be adamant that our relationship was over.

When a woman is pregnant I'm sure she lives with her pregnancy day by day, hour by hour, sometimes minute by minute. When a man is 200 miles away he has only his intuition and mine wasn't very good at the time. Maybe we had both turned our grief inward during the years of our marriage. She must have been handling some heavy stuff in her job and I was no help – I didn't know how to listen or how to ask the right questions. We had eventually drifted away from each other and divorced. Now, though, in 1999, one thing stood out for both of us – in our youth neither of us knew how to communicate.

I learned now that Carol had registered the birth in the hospital – she had been heavily sedated at the time – and I also learned that our son had arrived over two weeks early. That explained why I had been confused about dates. Thereafter, during our marriage, we were both terrified of getting pregnant again. That caused her to drift away from me. When we each stayed away from each other, we both interpreted it as the other having met someone else. She thought I had gone away to university to live with someone. I thought she was already virtually living with someone. We were both wrong.

Carol and I agreed to meet and talk. There was an obvious town equidistant from us both. I knew there was a market-place coffee-bar that would be easy to find. I phoned a friend for some advice.

'We need to meet somewhere quiet,' I said. 'And it needs to be a Saturday. Would that café-bar in the market-place be good?'

'Yes, I don't see why not,' he said. 'The town thins out later in the afternoon. It gets surprisingly quiet then.'

'What do you reckon? Say three-thirty?'

'I would say so.'

'Good. I'll suggest three-thirty in that market-place café.'

In my last letter before our first meeting in almost twenty-seven years I told Carol that I would get to the café early. She didn't like going into bars alone.

Turn right as you go in the café-bar and I'll be a few tables back, a clean-shaven fifty-year-old with short, swept-back fair hair (grey in places), wearing a pale blue shirt and cream trousers, and reading a copy of Bill Bryson's Notes from a Big Country. *I'll scout the town centre beforehand so we can move on to somewhere else if the café-bar is not suitable. Wherever we meet the back-cloth will probably be surreal.*

'So that's the basic story of the marriage,' I told Louise Archer, a few days before my meeting with Carol. We had varied our normal approach. This time I had read aloud what I'd written about my marriage to Carol.

'Thank you for that,' Louise said.

'No, thank you. It's my first public reading for a long time.'

'Should I have applauded at the end?'

'It's kind of you to even think about it.'

Louise clapped for all of two seconds.

'Looking back on it, getting married was such a weird thing to do,' I said.

'It's not that unusual for birth parents to marry each other later. If nothing else it legitimises the birth.'

'Maybe that was what we were doing.'

'Perhaps subconsciously. The baby is an incredibly binding life event. It's very emotionally connecting.'

'It certainly is.'

'Yes.'

'I wanted you to know the history of my marriage in case things go wrong when I meet Carol on Saturday. Then I can pick up with you again if I can't handle it on my own. I won't have to tell you the background.'

I was sitting next to a big bay window in the front room of Louise's house. I was being treated more like a guest than a client this time. The curtains were open and yet it felt very private and intimate because a privet hedge protected us from the street.

Suddenly a large cat jumped on the window ledge outside the house, a foot away from my chair. The cat startled me. Then I laughed.

'Did you train the cat so that it jumps on the window-sill to tell your clients that their time's up?' I asked.

Louise laughed without replying.

I stood up and reached for my bag.

'Whoa, wait a moment,' Louise said, holding her palm up to me. 'There's something I want to say.'

'Oh, sorry.'

I sat down again.

'Looking ahead to your meeting with Carol, I think the issue for you is that you are doing something alone that affects the lives of so many other people,' she said. 'You feel responsible for that. There's your son, his adoptive parents, his parents' siblings, maybe his partner, his partner's siblings, the birth mother, all her family members, and so on. You're starting something that may affect thirty or more people.'

I nodded, still sitting.

'It may change for you when you get more people on your side,' she added.

'Thank you,' I said. I stayed seated. Thought about it for a while. 'You're right. I'm worried about the effect on a whole array of people. I've been controlling this initiative and I'm in a position to trigger the emotions of so many others. I've had very little control through this saga and it feels very unnatural.'

'Where are you meeting Carol?' Louise asked.

'In a café-bar in the market-square at 3.30pm on Saturday. It's exactly halfway between where we live. It's also fifty yards from where we met for our first date.'

A friend of mine was doing a research project in Manchester. On the train journey to meet her for dinner I saw a young man wearing a T-shirt with the words GOD LOVES A TRIER.

'OK,' my friend said, after we had eaten. 'Here's an exercise for you. Describe me in five words and I'll describe you in five words.'

We found scraps of paper and serviettes and started thinking about what we might write.

'What is this?' I asked. 'Psycho-serviette-analysis?'

I wrote 'tall' and then searched for four more adjectives to describe my friend. I was used to a bigger canvas – an A4 pad rather than half a table napkin. She was the sort of woman who deserved a whole pack of napkins.

When she read back what she had written about me I was really surprised:

Funny.

Kind.

Sad.

Reliable.

Thoughtful/serious/wise/insightful.

The one that really surprised me was *sad*. I had seen myself that way at certain key times – during the aftermath of a relationship breakdown or when the loss of my son was particularly heartfelt – but now it made more sense to accept that I had a permanent core of sadness and loneliness. I'd always acknowledged to myself that I had a sadness deep down but I hadn't realised that others could see it. What also interested me was how most of the five character traits could be explained by one particular episode in my life. Losing a child was most of what was sad in my life. Losing a child gave me the tragic-comic humour needed to cope. Losing a child made me kinder to strangers than I might have been. Losing a child made me more dependable and responsible in the wake. And losing a child made me think more deeply than I might have otherwise.

Since the birth event, I had worked harder, thought more, and tried to take the role of the other. I had become a background character and I'd often punished myself by taking more challenging options rather than the easier routes. The search was a good example of a challenge. It was the hardest thing I'd ever done.

A few things went wrong during my hour-and-a-half bus journey to meet Carol for the first time in twenty-seven years. The bus was snarled up in holiday traffic and fell behind schedule. When a man with Tourette's Syndrome boarded the bus the driver lost patience with the man's swearing and wouldn't drive away until the man had got off.

I arrived in my market-place destination an hour and a half early rather than my planned two and a half hours. The café was buzzing and heaving with people. The tables outside and inside the café were swilling with lager and beer. Pint glasses took up most of the table-top space. A rock band was playing outside and the market-place was crowded. It was the world's worst setting for an intimate conversation.

Carol had a mobile-phone but I didn't. Even if I looked around and tried to find a better venue we couldn't contact each other. I had anticipated the day to be surreal and it had lived up to my expectation.

Fortunately the band stopped playing twenty minutes before our meeting and the people thinned out just enough for me to find a seat in the café. I moved nearer the door when another table came vacant.

We recognised each other immediately. Carol looked as though she had already had a hard day. It took ten minutes before we composed ourselves.

'Why have you brought it all up again?' she asked.

Our conversation began. We talked for an hour and then walked and talked for another hour. We added to the stories of the birth and our relationship. We caught up on what had happened since. Both her parents were still alive. Mine, of course, were dead.

By the end of the meeting we were both drained. Carol held herself together very well while we were together but she told me later that she was in floods of tears as soon as she was out of my sight. On my return journey I stared blurry-eyed through a bus window as thirty-one years of my life passed before me by like trees on the roadside. Where did it all go? What happened to those years? What happened to our son?

The next day I felt very low in energy, and my back was aching. The build-up to the meeting had taken a lot out of Carol and me, and we both got chest infections that summer. But I was also pleased because Louise had got it right. I did feel better now that Carol was involved. Indeed the search became a little easier from this point. It felt less daunting now there were two of us with a shared goal. Carol was content to move the search forward when the time was right for her. I understood that she had to take whatever time she needed. I had to wait for her to catch up.

On reflection both Carol and I thought that the meeting had gone amazingly well. Overall it felt like an achievement. We were both dealing with something that had hung around too long without being resolved. In our next exchange of letters we forgave each other for what had happened. I preferred to dwell on our joint bravery at facing each other after all these years rather than our anger and pain at the time. We had to give ourselves credit for overcoming such a trauma, getting on with our lives and making the best of them.

Nan, my search buddy, travelled out of her way to meet me. We went for a walk in the hills with her dog. There seemed little progress in our searches, but we agreed that this could be the calm before the storm. We were driving ourselves forward and Nan's can-do attitude lifted me. Somehow she would get to Japan; somehow I would meet my son.

20

Secrets and synchronicities

'My wife and I have decided not to have any children,' Roger told me one day when my birth son was three and a half. Roger was a work colleague of mine in the days I was married. He was a man I admired, a few years older than me, a real mentor. 'We've both got good jobs and it would take away our freedom. How about you and Carol? Are you going to have children?'

'I don't know,' I said.

Carol and I hadn't talked about children since our bad experience. We hadn't talked about it before our first experience either.

I looked at my friend and realised that I felt safe and relaxed. We had played tennis in the morning and watched the FA Cup Final in the afternoon. Roger had cooked a meal for me. We were drinking and talking.

'We're not getting on very well at the moment,' I admitted.

'I'm sorry,' he said.

'I haven't seen her much recently.'

'Is it something that can be solved?' my friend asked.

I told him more of the story. I told him that there had been a baby. It was the first time I had told anyone the tale. Since the adoption I felt as though I had signed away my right to tell the truth. When I got home that night I felt like a spy who had sold secrets and betrayed his country. But it was a step forward. Finally. Three and a half years had passed since the birth. Three and a half years of silence on the subject.

I went on my own to see a marriage guidance counsellor. I told the counsellor some of the story. She asked me questions about the marriage and there were some I couldn't answer.

'I often do work with one person from within the marriage,' she told me, 'but in this case I think it would be important to see both of you. Would your wife be willing to come?'

'I don't know.'

I went away meaning to ask my wife if she could come with me to the counsellor. Maybe I asked her, maybe I didn't. But we didn't go as a couple. We didn't talk about it together. We didn't solve the problem.

While I was a university student I told the story about the baby three or four times to friends. After each tale-telling I stayed awake long into the night. My head buzzed with the details…and yet I knew so few details. Each time I released my pent-up narrative I waited for a meteorite to strike me down and a newspaper front page to batter me with its headlines. Each time I told the story, however, the person kept my trust and gifted me empathy. I think I already knew enough to select people who had experienced life, people who had known some pain themselves.

When I told the story my listeners were often surprised by two things:

'You were so young.'

'I don't understand why you got married later.'

When my biological son was eight I travelled around Britain with Kathy and Sandra, two friends from Canada. In Wales, we went to the smallest house in Britain (in Conway) and spent a few days in Bangor. Sandra claimed a hat trick as she had now been to Bangor (Maine), Bangor (Wales) and Bangor (Northern Ireland).

On New Year's Eve we went to a pantomime and were surprised to find that it was all in Welsh. The only bits we understood were

'Oh yes we will, oh no we won't' and a bucket of paper being thrown over the audience. When the cast took their bows at the end we were amazed to discover that one character was a villain rather than a hero. Afterwards we drank in a Bangor pub and came out tipsy, shouting 'Happy New Year, Newfoundland' across the sea.

On one train journey Kathy sat next to a man who was reading a television drama script. Kathy looked across at one point and a line jumped out from the script.

'It said, *What are we going to do about the baby?*' Kathy told us after the man had left the train.

Later that evening, I told her about my adopted baby and she told me about hers.

'I went into a mother-and-baby home,' Kathy said. 'When I came out it was back to normal. I was still seeing the guy. We were still screwing around.' She shook her head. 'It caught up with me later.'

I met Joan through my girlfriend Elaine when my son was twelve. Joan was an Australian in her mid-twenties. She was visiting England and making contact with what she called her blood father. Since meeting Ruby I'd thought of myself as a biological father but Joan gave me this new name – blood father.

'I walked in the house and his wife called him from upstairs,' Joan told Elaine and me. 'He came down the stairs and I couldn't believe it. Here was this really young man, a really handsome man, coming down to greet me. My parents are so much older. They're from a different generation.'

I wondered if anyone would ever turn up on my doorstep, thrust a can of Foster's into my hand and say, 'G'day, Dad, so you're a journo, eh?'

When my son was thirteen I won a short-story competition. First prize was a week at writers' summer school. My friends reckoned that second prize had to be two weeks. During the week of my prize

I met a writer who was an adoptive mother. It was like crossing to the other side, sitting with rival fans at a derby match.

'How old are your children?' I asked her over dinner one night. I could feel my stomach fluttering.

She told me and I did the arithmetic.

Not mine.

I exhaled for the first time since asking the question.

We shared more of our adoption stories.

'There's never a day goes by without me being thankful for the presence of my children,' she said.

'Thank you for saying that,' I said. Her comment appealed to my altruistic side. Maybe our gift had helped others.

'It's true,' she said.

'Do your children ever want to know more about their background?'

'They always seem most interested in what I say when I talk about their origins.'

Origins?

I was my son's original father as well as being his real father, genetic father, biological father and blood father. This was back in the days when I hadn't yet heard the term birth father.

I was shocked to discover that this woman was separated from her husband. I had assumed that the marriages of adoptive couples lasted forever. I thought the adoption agency had checked couples thoroughly for their solidity, security and marital longevity.

'I found out that he was having affairs with foreign students,' she told me. 'I often wonder how men who adopt children might feel about their virility.'

'I'll think about that one for a few years,' I said.

I stayed in touch with my new friend. Soon afterwards, in her late-forties, she became pregnant and added to her adoptive children with one of her own blood. I gained some consolation from the pleasure she obviously found in her children. People who adopt children must be really special people, I thought. They must really want their children. They must really love them.

It was only years later that I realised that it wasn't only about wanting their children and loving them, it was also about adopting children because they weren't able to get children any other way. Adoption was their way of projecting a family to the world. Some of them may have been desperate for a child.

I occasionally revisited the issue of virility and fertility. What if one adoptive parent was fertile and the other one wasn't? Might the fertile one have gone along with the other's wishes to adopt? Might the adoption bring out the fertile one's desire to produce a child of their own? And might the fertile one then go off to form a new relationship? The adoption equation wasn't only complex from my viewpoint. It was complex from everyone's viewpoint.

My son was fifteen when my flat-mate introduced me to a friend of his who was doing a PhD on issues affecting the adoption of black children into white families. I thought her work was fascinating. To me it confirmed that adoption was still at the experimental stage. Lots of long-term evaluation was still needed.

My flat-mate's friend gave me the name of an organisation – British Agencies for Adoption and Fostering – and I wrote the name in my notebook. I included no address or phone number for the agency. It was nothing much really, except that it showed that I was registering something about the world of adoption.

Another flat-mate of mine in Oxford worked as a residential social worker. While we were sharing the flat he launched a successful business as a photographer. His first paid photography job was taking pictures of children who were being put up for fostering and adoption.

21

Autumn 1999

Carol and I arranged a second meeting and we agreed the wording of a letter for our son's Social Services file. We needed some idle time though. There was such a lot to process. Carol's parents were still against us initiating contact with our son. It was easier for me to move forward because I no longer had to take my parents' views into account. On the other hand there were times when I wished that I had taken the initiative while they were still alive.

Carol was concerned. She hoped that our birth son had had a good childhood and education and had by now got a good career and a good standard of living. If he hadn't, she thought that it might add to her guilt for letting him go for adoption. I felt the same way.

Twenty years ago I had lived with Elaine in Cambridge. Now Elaine was very ill. When I told her about meeting Carol again she was pleased that I was searching for some resolution. In a letter Elaine remembered that my loss had interfered with our relationship: *Such a heartbreaking experience to have gone through so young. It has really coloured/affected your life since.*

Two months after our first meeting Carol and I met in a Peak District café. We signed the letter to Social Services and agreed on a method of approach to the list of people with our son's name. But we delayed the actual approach. There were other things to do first. First we wanted to meet the social worker and look at the relevant parts of our son's adoption file.

It was almost a year since my awkward meeting with the woman from Social Services. Carol and I now wrote to the social worker, who acknowledged receipt of our letters and called up the adoption file for a second time. She also wanted us to explain our purpose.

In my next letter to the social worker I explained how we wanted to contact our birth son through an intermediary, look at aspects of the file relevant to us, ensure that all correspondence post-1996 was kept in a separate file, and hand over the letter we'd written to our birth son so that it could go on file in case he ever looked at the file. I felt as though I always had to justify my actions.

I received a reply: *It will be possible for you to read any personal information relating to yourselves, and I will contact you to arrange a convenient date, time and venue. Your recent contacts will remain confidential in a separate file.*

But the social worker was still pushing the NORCAP route: *It would also be important for us to discuss at this meeting if you would wish to consider further, a non-disclosure agreement with NORCAP, who could trace on your behalf.*

Eleven days later she wrote again, pleased to inform us that our birth son's adoption records had been relocated. A meeting was arranged. We would see the relevant parts of the file.

I spoke with Louise Archer on the telephone.

'What might we have to deal with when we look at the file?' I asked.

'It varies enormously,' she told me. 'There may not be much. But there should be notes of your meetings with the authorities.'

'But it's worth seeing the file?'

'I think so. It's important because some adoptees are just handed the file, having turned down offers of counselling, and any errors in the file can have consequences. Sometimes individual judgments are on the file. It might stop the adoptee from going forward.'

'I take your point.'

'When you do find the file, it can be disconcerting to see bits of it Tippexed out so that you can't see them,' Louise said. 'Different Social Services may have different stances on how they exercise confidentiality. You're also dealing with bureaucracies. Some parts of bureaucracies can be cold, blunt or sterile.'

'And we're dealing with people within them.'

'Yes. There can be egos involved in the adoption business.'

'As everywhere.'

'As everywhere.'

'I need to warn you that there may be some disturbing things in the file,' the social worker told Carol and me. She had greeted us cordially and was sitting across the table from us in a stark meeting room. 'I can leave you with the relevant pages and come back in a little while.'

Carol had taken a day off work and it meant another day trip for me. In the build-up to the meeting Carol and I had agreed that the file would offer an invaluable refresher course as there was so much that we couldn't remember about the trauma. We had to meet the official agents, the type of people who had taken our son away from us and hurt us in an enduring way, but we were also inching closer to our son.

The social worker left the room and we started to read through the pages from our past. Carol and I read the case history at a similar pace. Her parents were described in terms of their build, eye colour, religion, siblings, education, jobs, parents' jobs and type of house. I was astonished that my father's job was listed so specifically (*his father is a football manager*). I thought it was very easy to identify my family from the information in the file.

We read the next part of the report.

As everything has been kept very secret regarding the pregnancy and a marriage out of the question, an adoption is hoped for. No member of the family, neighbours or friends know of the pregnancy.

The description of me was based solely on the interview with the church social worker thirty-one years before.

He is described as an intelligent boy, rather shy and very ashamed of what has happened.

Carol and I were ready to turn the page at the same time.

When it came to the description of the baby we both shook our heads when we saw the words *normal delivery*. We knew that wasn't correct.

Then Carol spoke aloud.

'He didn't have odd ears,' she said. 'That's rubbish.'

I read the next piece of the report:

Mr B [the foster father] said that he is quite a normal baby in every way except for odd ears. One is perfectly formed (the right one), and lies close to his head, but the left one is curled forward and sticks out.

'That simply isn't true,' Carol said. 'I visited him at six weeks and he was perfect.'

We pointed together at the report as we reached the line saying that Carol's father had been *most anxious to give the [diocesan] council [for social work] a cheque in appreciation of all the help we have given.*

I looked at the letter-headed notepaper. The president of the agency was a bishop. The chairman was another bishop. The case was dealt with by a church social worker.

We turned over the page and found a reference for me from my family doctor.

I know his family well. There is no evidence of hereditary disease, emotional or nervous instability, or in fact anything at all.

Carol and I laughed aloud at exactly the same time.

No evidence of…anything at all.

There was a summary of my interview with the social worker.

He was anxious to help, rather shy and ashamed. No question of marriage. They do not see each other now.

That was yet another error in the report.

No question of marriage.

Then Carol and I read that the initiative to move the adoption to another county had come from Carol's parents. The file contained a comment that her parents had proved difficult. But I thought it was sensible not to settle for a local adoption. If your grandson has to disappear out of your reach would you want him reading the same local newspaper as yourself, riding the same buses, buying petrol from the next pump to yours and going to the same school as you had?

Next in the file came a letter written to Carol by the adoption caseworker six weeks after the birth. It explained a little about the home that our son was going to.

We know you would like to hear something of the adopters we have chosen. They are a happily married couple who have been quite unable to have children of their own, but they are so fond of children they decided to have their family by adoption.

The adoptive parents were described in terms of school, jobs, parents' jobs, siblings' jobs and hobbies. There was almost enough information for me to have tracked them down.

'Look at my signature,' Carol said when we looked at the consent form.

'Is that your signature?' I asked.

'It doesn't look anything like it, does it?'

'Not a bit.'

It looked like it had been scrawled by a spider in a dark filing cabinet. It could have been written by someone with a broken hand as well as a broken heart.

The social worker returned to the room.

'Could we photocopy a few pages, please?' I asked.

'Yes. Of course.'

The social worker photocopied five pages for us. Then we discussed what we might do from here. It was a more relaxed conversation. I didn't feel as though we were overpowered. The social worker was now accepting of Louise Archer's role. We made it clear that we would handle the situation sensitively.

We gave the social worker the letter that Carol and I had compiled before the meeting. She promised to put it in the file so that our birth son could see it if he ever looked at his file. In the letter we said how we had never forgotten him and would be very receptive if he ever wished to make contact with us. This could be done through our experienced intermediary who could explain more of the situation.

Slowly, we were releasing the burden.

Now we needed to slow down. Everything was happening too quickly.

Louise Archer and I arranged to meet in an Arts Centre coffee-bar in a small town that was accessible for us both. On my journey I saw a woman with a meaningful T-shirt: CHILDREN SHOULD BE HERDED BUT NOT SEEN.

The Arts Centre was a mid-range venue featuring rising stars. A poster showed that Kate Rusby was coming soon. Louise had said that the coffee-bar would be empty at this time of day and she was perfectly correct. It was also dark, secluded and spooky. I could hardly see what I was writing in my notebook. When Louise arrived she had difficulty recognising me.

'Is it you?' she asked tentatively.

'It is me,' I said.

We laughed at our ridiculous conversation.

When seated with coffees I told Louise the story of meeting the social worker. She was angry when I mentioned the donation from Carol's parents.

'I think agencies sometimes got donations from both sides,' she said. 'Some adoptive parents used to send donations to the agency every year.'

'I was surprised at the medical reports.'

'Yes. Right down to the tests for sexually transmitted diseases.'

'Carol needs some more time. Shall we let you know when we are ready for you to start contacting the names on the list?'

'I don't do any searches in the two months surrounding Christmas,' she said. 'It's a time of too much emotion and people don't always make the best decisions around that time.'

'I know,' I said. 'I've learned not to make important decisions in

January.'

Carol and I would wait until we were both ready, whether it was late-January or mid-August. We had to be strong enough to face the possibility of rejection. Both Carol and I harboured fears that he might reject us.

I showed Louise the letter describing the adoptive family.

'The PR for the families was amazing,' she said. 'This was a fantasy family.'

'And like job applications it may or may not be true.'

'The reality could not match the fantasy.'

'I guess everything was relatively unknown about the adoptive parents. I can't imagine the church using private detectives to check that the adoptive parents were bona fide, or putting "No wife-beaters should apply" on the application form.'

'I don't like the sound of the adoptive mother being adopted herself,' Louise said.

'Why not?' I asked.

'It's almost as though it seems like it's the norm of how you have children.'

'How do you mean?'

'If the mother hasn't done her own tracing, what sort of messages does that send out? Also, it sends out messages about how you have children.'

I went quiet. My father had been adopted.

'Yeah, that happened in my family,' I said. 'Because my father was adopted, I thought that adopting children was all right. It wasn't until later that I realised how much fall-out there was.'

'Oh,' Louise said.

'How do you think it plays out here?'

'Some adoptive parents may see no need for searching. If he was searching just for himself then it might have happened earlier. Some search and some don't. But here you've got two generations of people who may or may not search.'

'Maybe the message is "I know that I'm adopted but that is as far as it goes",' I said.

'Searching could reinforce the fears that children are taken away. That's a fear that adoptive parents have – that birth parents come on the scene and they lose their children. It's just that the adoptive mother being adopted gives you more to think about. It's not as straightforward as before.'

'It makes my life more complicated too.'

'Because your father was adopted?'

'Yes.'

'Have you written about your father's adoption.'

'A little. I wrote a book about my father's life as it was before I had been born. In that book I looked at how parts of his life had played out in mine. His adoption was part of the story so I included it.'

'Could you do a little writing about your father's adoption for me?'

'Yes.'

'I think it's very relevant.'

'How?'

'I don't know. Maybe curiosity about how babies are made.'

'All right, I'll do that while I'm waiting for Carol to give me the go-ahead. We're almost ready to move forward to the letters.'

'When you're ready I'll write to the names on our list one at a time and wait for a reply until I try the next.'

'No multiple letters?'

'No. If I sent five letters all at once I wouldn't know which one was replying or phoning, would I?'

'True,' I said. I let out a sigh.

'How are you coping with all this?' Louise asked.

'It's exciting and scary. And the outcome's uncertain.'

'You've prepared well. You're as ready for it as you can be.'

'The whole adoption system is a kaleidoscope of uncertainty, right from the point of "Shall we keep the child or let him go?," I said. 'Then it escalates into more and more uncertainty. Is the child having a good or bad upbringing? Is this the child? Is that the child? Right down to answering that question about whether I have any children. But maybe not every birth father has the confusion that I have. Some people probably close it down and become more rigid and dogmatic about their answers.'

'Some people construct other sorts of lifestyles so they can hide it from themselves,' Louise added. 'But it never goes away. It is always likely to resurface.'

'I know, I know.'

My search buddy, Nan, phoned me with great excitement. Her film company had been awarded a contract in Japan, and she would be the production manager for the job. Nan had set to work organising a director, a cameraman and actors for a drinks-company film. She'd developed shooting schedules to suit the light and arranged general views (GVs) of Tokyo. In the midst of that, for the first time in her career, she'd created a day off while on location. She planned to travel for an hour and meet her half-brother and his family for lunch.

Three of us – Carol, Louise and myself – looked separately at the list of people in Britain with the same name as the man we were looking for. We had already reduced the address-list to thirty-seven people of the same name. Now we ruled out those who shared a surname with a woman at the same address (because Louise knew that our son hadn't married in Britain). This reduced the list to eleven. These we ranked in some kind of order. Having gone through the process independently we found that the three of us had put the same address at the top of the list.

I tried to think of other canny ways to refine this list of people with the same name as my son. Could I find the age bands of these men by phoning friends who worked in marketing companies and therefore had access to mailing lists? Should I go to the electoral registers and see if any names on the list had been there longer than thirteen years (before my son was eighteen) so that I could rule them out? Should I ask two friends of mine who had the same surname as my son if they had any relatives with his first name?

In the end I didn't do any of those things; they all felt too intrusive. But I did look up his name in all the major professional directories – vicars, doctors, solicitors, politicians, publishers, etc – without finding a match. There was one professional footballer of exactly the same name, but he had been born two years after my son. That would have been a wonderful circular dénouement as my father had been a professional footballer.

Our list of names included one person who lived with nine others at an address in a poor area of Liverpool. I guessed that this was either a hostel or some other multiple occupancy. Soon afterwards, when I was in Liverpool, I looked up this address in the electoral registers and found that he had been living there for the past five years. Four of the people in the house had Germanic names. I hoped this man of the same name wasn't our son but I knew we had to be prepared for anything.

Another one of the same name lived in a university hall of residence in a northern city. Maybe he was a mature student (as I had once been). Maybe he had settled for the safe sanctuary of a hall of residence so that he could work harder (as I had once done). I wouldn't mind if it was him.

Another lived in an address with eight other men in a small northern town. Again this looked like multiple occupancy. Spare us this one, please, I thought. It was bringing up all my prejudices.

I had friends who lived near to some of the addresses on the list. Could I ask some of my friends to check out the house? Again I decided not to. Again it was too compromising.

Around the same time a friend of mine came across someone in uniform at London's Euston Station. She looked at the young man's name badge and saw that his Christian name and surname matched the ones I sought.

She phoned me and told me about this serendipity.

'And you're sure it wasn't him?' I asked.

'It wasn't him,' she said. 'He was no more than twenty. Nowt but a bairn.'

It wasn't only Carol and I who were searching. My close friends were doing it too.

He had to be somewhere on our list.

Unless he was sleeping rough.

Unless he was living abroad.

Unless, unless, unless…

Nan phoned me to debrief after her trip to Japan. She had spent time with her half-brother and his family while dealing with the usual vicissitudes of filming. She talked about her half-brother's hair, ears, eyes and mannerisms. She promised to show me her photographs at the earliest possible moment.

I couldn't have wished for a more inspiring search buddy than Nan.

22

My father's adoption

'What was it like being adopted?' I asked my father as our family threesome travelled by car to my Uncle Bill's house in Worcestershire. I had recently returned from spending the summer with Ruby in Kentucky, and I was determined to spend more time with my parents and learn more about them.

'I think I got away with things that the others didn't,' my father said. 'If Bill got caught pinching apples he'd get a good clout round the ear. If I got caught, I'd get told off.'

'Did you ever want to know about your real parents?'

'When I grew a bit older I knew who my mother was. Someone would occasionally point her out from a distance. But I kept away from my mother as much as I could, in case they fetched me back. That was in the back of my mind. She'd married a chappie who lived a couple of miles away. He came up to me one day and talked to me.'

'What did you talk about?'

'He talked about football when I started playing for Charlton Kings. I knew nothing about the family.'

'You never met your mother?' I asked.

'No.'

'You knew her name?'

'She was called Ruby Ward before she married the chappie.'

'Ruby?' I said. 'Like my American girlfriend's name?'

'Yes.'

'Well, that's a coincidence.'

We all nodded. I looked at my mother in the back seat.

Had I married my American Ruby, had she taken my surname, she would have been Ruby Ward, the same as the maiden name of my Dad's biological mother. I needed a flowchart to understand this one.

'Your father could have been any nationality, Tim,' my mother said. 'He could have been a sailor.'

My father nodded, wistfully. That was true. He knew who his real mother was, but not his real father.

'Do you think he was Brazilian?' I asked. 'You might have got your football skills from him rather than your mum.'

My father looked pensive. He was very proud of having played football for England and didn't want to consider his father not being English.

'The most amazing thing was that my name was never changed,' he said. 'I didn't know until about seven or eight years ago that you could change your name overnight.'

'That is amazing,' I agreed.

'The big worry always at the back of my mind was that my mum was coming to take me back,' my father continued. 'If the real mother has had a rough time and wants someone then it's always a possibility. One occasion, the first time I played football for Cheltenham Boys, the officials of the schoolboy team wanted to see my birth certificate. I asked a teacher where I could find my birth certificate and he said my mother would have it. I thought he meant my real mother. By then I knew where my real mother and her husband lived so I went to their home. It was a farmhouse about two miles away. I walked to the house and then walked up and down outside for perhaps half an hour. I remember walking up and down, thinking what a stupid thing it was, having to knock on the door and ask for my birth certificate from someone I didn't know. I didn't know what I could say if someone answered the door. Eventually I thought, Bugger it, I won't play. I told the teachers I didn't have a birth certificate. They said I could play anyway.'

'Did you talk to anybody about being adopted?' I asked.

'I kept away from the subject as much as I could. The other kids used to tell me that they'd come and take me away. I never talked about it after I went into football. It was a different time. It was a black mark against you. You kept as quiet as you could. People weren't as broadminded as they are now. They would take it out on you.'

'Mmm,' I said. 'The kids knew you were born out of wedlock because your surname was different to that of your brothers.'

My father nodded.

'The majority of people were decent people,' he said. 'The kids at school could be cruel without thinking about it. In my day the kids with glasses were called "Foureyes".'

At this point in my life I didn't understand why my father's surname hadn't been changed. Later I presumed it was because his adoption was informal and had taken place before the Adoption Act 1926.

I turned to my mother.

'Did it worry you, Mum, that he was adopted?' I asked.

'No, it never bothered me,' she said, leaning forward in the car. 'My brother had a friend called Arthur Curtis who'd been brought up by an aunt. I think that helped me to understand.'

'You had a lot to deal with, too, Nancy,' my father said.

My mother went quiet and looked a little tearful.

'My dad was a brute,' she told me. 'He was in the 1914 War. He used to bring his pals home and they used to make home-brew and it used to give them the blues. They used to try to climb the walls. Then they'd get fighting.'

'What was your mother like?' I asked her.

'She had some fine qualities but she was quick-tempered. She eloped with him at eighteen. She was determined to beat her parents. Grandma wrote to churches in the area to try to stop the wedding. My father was a horror. He would beat Mother. I've seen him with a carving knife at Mother's throat. They had some flaming rows. Mother would have to cover her eyes up a lot. She'd have black eyes. Mother was a nervous wreck. She went to see a solicitor and got a court order.'

'How old were you then?'

'They separated when I was about ten. I could have been younger, eight or nine.'

'Did you stay in touch with him?' I asked.

'He might come with a few presents at Christmas. Then Mother shut him off.'

'Did he pay maintenance?'

'Sometimes he paid, sometimes he didn't. Mother got a job. We lived OK. It was a struggle but we were always well dressed.'

'And then your father died quite young?' I asked.

'Tim was on leave when we got a telegram to say that Father had been found drowned,' my mother continued. 'They couldn't understand it. Then we found out that he'd committed bigamy. They'd never divorced; Mother wouldn't divorce him. He'd married the girl and we think there was a baby, which was why he'd probably married her.'

Aha. I finally understood one of the running jokes in my nuclear family. Whenever we passed a prison my dad would ask my mum if she wanted to call in and see any of her relatives. My mum would laugh and turn to me and say 'Isn't he awful?'

'Father could be good company,' my mother told me now. 'He could fool about and have you helpless with laughter. He was a hard worker. He worked at the railway and helped move scenery at the Hippodrome in the evenings. He used to help a friend with his greyhounds to get some spare money but he didn't always give the money to Mother.'

Years later I thought about my parents and Carol's parents. The four of them had lost a grandchild. What was that like? Had they talked to anyone about it?

'I'm really sorry that I haven't brought you any grandchildren,' I told my parents one day.

'That's no problem,' my father said. 'We just adopt other people's children and play with them.'

I looked at my mother. She looked upset.

I couldn't find the words or the strength to talk about it any more. We had talked about my father's adoption…but not about the other adoption.

I was with both my parents when they died and I certainly grieved for them, but overall I found coping with the loss of my son harder than dealing with my parents' deaths. My son's disappearance was a loss without a body, and I didn't see it happening. When you lose a child to the adoption process there is no ceremony, no name, no funeral and no finality. After talking to my father about his adoption I also felt his real mother's loss and wondered who my dad's original father was.

After my dad's death I asked my Uncle Bill if he remembered anything about my father's origins.

'I was about five at the time,' Uncle Bill said. 'I think Tim was about six months old when he came to us. Our mother brought him home and laid him on the settee. Our father came home from his job at the railway and sat on him.'

Some years after my father's death I realised something very significant – I was the only blood relative that my father ever met.

23

Winter 1999–2000

Louise, Carol and I agreed on the wording for a letter that Louise would send to the people with the same name as our birth son. A lot of thought went into that letter. Louise would ask the person to reply even if he wasn't the person we were seeking. A stamped-and-addressed envelope was included. Everybody had to be ready. It could all happen very quickly when the letters began to go out. Well, we hoped things might happen quickly.

Another Christmas approached. In the build-up I saw a woman wearing a T-shirt with a message: ALL MY XMAS PRESENTS ARE HOMEMADE – YOU'RE GETTING MY CHILDREN.

Another Christmas passed with my usual feelings of loss. Carol and I spent months preparing ourselves. Sometimes we just needed time to go by.

One day I studied the numbers of adoptions and the proportion of adopted children who do search. The number of searches seemed incredibly small. I decided that it took an exceptional set of circumstances for an adopted child to search for a birth father.

I concluded that putting a letter in the NORCAP file and joining the national register were virtually useless from my point of view. I wrote a few words in my notebook: *The trouble with the system is that it is more weighted down with guidelines and rules, all put there for good reason, but it doesn't work out well.*

It would have cost me £30 to register on the national register. I reckoned the odds were one in a thousand of a hit. It wasn't worth a £30 gamble at this stage of the search.

I met Louise in a Peak District café. It was two o'clock and the lunchtime rush had barely died. The counter-waitress held her head with her hands.

'Hard day?' I asked.

She looked at me.

'You just can't find good management any more,' she said. 'What can I get you?'

A few minutes later I took two coffees back to our table.

'I've been looking at flats for sale,' I told Louise.

'Are you thinking of buying somewhere?'

'Yes. But I need help. I look at places with only one thing in mind.'

'What's that?'

'Where I would put my desk and work table. I like to get a feel for where I'd work. I don't see the rest of the place, except for where I might bang my head.'

'I've always visualised you at your desk.'

I looked at Louise. We had a very relaxed relationship. Boundaries, I thought. Respect the boundaries. Louise was in my life to teach me how to keep sensible boundaries.

'I don't know what to write about next,' I told Louise. 'Have you got any ideas?'

'Let me think for a moment.'

'I was thinking about writing about myself as an outsider.'

'I think you covered that when you discussed authority.'

'I'm thinking more of how I react to call-centres and answering trees. They alienate me so much that I begin to hear "Your call is important to us" as "Your call is impotent to us". I only vote to save someone else stealing my vote, and I can't identify with mass-media stories. I value my independence but recognise that if I live alone I can become very detached from society. But I also know that others feel detached too – more and more people are living alone and freelancing – so I'm thinking about writing a book called *The Disconnected Citizen*. I've put it on my list of books that I might or might not ever write.'

'Do you feel you've covered everything about the impact of being a birth father?'

'I don't know.'

'There is one other thing I thought about.'

'What's that?'

'Well, I'm interested in the development of your sexual confidence. Your relationships with Irene and Valerie sound as though they were cemented through highly-charged sex, but your relationship with Carol was surrounded by shame and secrecy. How did you get from one place to the other?'

'I don't know. I think I had a lot of help.'

'Well, it was just an idea.'

'It's the best I've heard so far. The adoption incident left me with a deeply-rooted melancholia but I've still had some wonderful relationships.'

'That is something to write about.'

Ten weeks after Christmas, Carol phoned to say that she was ready to go ahead. She also had a tale of synchronicity to tell me.

'When I first got the letter from Louise I knew exactly what it was,' Carol told me. 'It threw me into a real spin. During the next few weeks I had an appointment with my solicitor about something else and I asked her about this. The solicitor clarified for me that the search was legal. Then she asked me a few questions. She seemed eager for me to do the search. Well, I saw her again last week and it turns out that she'd been adopted and is searching for her own birth mother.'

24

Sex, shame and safety

I met Lesley when I was nearly halfway through my degree and beginning to lose my staid look. I had long straight hair, combed forward over my forehead and sideways over my ears and a big bushy beard that I washed often and trimmed rarely.

Lesley was a little older than the average student and therefore closer to my age. But she'd lived a more active life than me and seemed older and more worldly. Our lives were rarely synchronised in the fifteen months we were together. During term-time Lesley felt too close and clingy for my comfort. She was unhappy on campus, homesick and yearning for a practical life rather than an intellectual one. During short vacations I made my parents' house a base while Lesley returned to a busy hometown life which included an exciting job and a boyfriend. She was always glad to be away from university whereas I was always glad to be there.

During the periods we were apart, however, Lesley set a prototype for me about how communication was possible. During vacations she wrote me long letters that didn't hold anything back. Her letters both thrilled and shocked me. In return I tried to become more honest in the written word. Until I met Lesley I didn't realise that people could talk about intimate matters, let alone write about them.

She also taught me that bodies could be enjoyable rather than dangerous. I carried a lot of sexual guilt but her hedonistic sexual impulses gave me a better perspective. Even so I didn't want her to stay overnight; I didn't want anyone to sense what I was doing. Sex still felt taboo.

'It's OK, I want it too,' she reminded me one time, when I seemed to be holding back.

A week after the start of one university term Lesley knocked on my door late one evening carrying a bottle of Southern Comfort. It was the first time I had seen her for weeks. She had been home during the vacation and had been reluctant to return to university. She poured out two glasses of hooch and her troubles.

'I'm a week late and I don't care,' she told me.

I started thinking about what her pregnancy might mean. Oh, no, the father could be me. I had seen her a few weeks ago.

'I'm a week late and I don't care,' she repeated.

What if someone else was the father and she wanted to keep the child? Would I take on the child as my way of making amends? Having already given up a child to another couple, would I now take on a child fathered by someone else? Was this the way the system worked – no-one ends up with the right child?

'I'm a week late for the start of term and I don't care,' she repeated.

Oh.

'So you're not pregnant,' I said.

'What are you talking about?'

'I thought you were pregnant.'

'No, of course not.'

'Oh.'

'I'm just not sure I'm motivated enough to carry on with this degree.'

We laughed about the misunderstanding later.

In my second year at university I kept a diary for six months. The entries give no indication of a troubled man. The diary is a vibrant log of study, play and people. It has an undercurrent of excitement. It reads like the diary of a young man looking forward to the future. But at one point I confronted the issue of having (or not having) children: *At the moment the way I feel is that all my reasons for wanting children are bad ones – the immortal narcissism (i.e. wanting to see yourself live on), wanting someone to look after you when you reach old age, wanting an object to turn authority on, something to mould. Besides, I'm not sure it's going to be much fun being around in another twenty years.*

If I did mention my past trauma I put a positive slant on it, like my number-three reason for going to university: *Obviously the personal problems – the desire to run? I tend to like to think of it as the desire to face the world again.*

But the signs of psychological trouble were clearly there when I reflected on one long conversation with Lesley: *When talking with her I tend to reminisce somewhat – start noticing that I'm going through it all again when going to bed, start dreaming of bumping into everyone again.*

I rejoined the world while writing that diary. Re-reading it I can see my confidence returning. I had met lots of people at university and was enjoying life. I had lots of female friends, although Lesley was the only one I slept with. When I revisited my work colleagues during vacations they said how much I had changed. My confidence was slowly returning.

My relationship with Lesley continued through my last year at university. She still had her hometown boyfriend and I had my vacation vacancy. We connected over shallow word-play and deep conversation, jokes and analysis, travel and ideas, psychology and sociology, reading and writing. But Lesley lived in the here and now, and I lived in the past and future.

Once she settled in to a new term Lesley wanted to be with me every night but I wanted to keep pretences of respectability. In my final year I lived in a student room next to a discreet back door. If Lesley stayed overnight she could slip out that door, sneak through the hedge-lined path and be on the road without anyone noticing. Lesley didn't mind being seen, of course. It was me who wanted concealment. I was presenting a celibate, respectable image of myself. I lived my life as if a private detective was watching me and looking for evidence under an extinct Divorce Act. In the process I made Lesley feel like a servant girl. I took the shame of my first sexual relationship through the second. It wasn't that I didn't respect her; I just didn't respect myself for being sexual.

Lesley had another year of university to do after I graduated. At one point I seriously thought of applying for a one-year post with the Student Union in order to remain in town and stay with her. I also considered learning a trade, but my dominant plan was to secure a place at a North American university for further study. I worked on my scheme for eighteen months, collecting information, visiting one Canadian campus while travelling and making a detailed application. When everything fell into place for my Canadian venture I followed that route and Lesley and I parted as friends. I didn't realise that I'd been in love with Lesley until it took me a year to get over her. I had turned twenty-six when I left university but felt too raw to enter a rest-of-life relationship. Lesley was only the second person I'd slept with. Thereafter the numbers escalated and the relationships grew more and more confusing, especially the parts of those relationships that touched on reproduction issues.

Three years later, when my son was nine, I worked with a woman called Christine in Nottingham. My desk rested against hers and our chairs faced each other. She had fine straight hair that draped neatly as she worked. When she looked up she showed me a cute smile. Her legs lasted for ever, stretching under the desk, and occasionally our feet brushed as we slumped in our chairs. We had both spent time in Liverpool, so we often slipped into Merseyside talk.

'This Liverpudlian got on a bus…'

'At Pier 'Ed?'

'At Pier 'Ed. And this fellah says to the conductor, "Is this bus going to Speke?" And the conductor says, "I've been on it all day, lah, and it hasn't said a word."'

Christine and I enjoyed looking into each other's eyes from two desk-widths away, enjoyed it so much that we eventually decided to shorten the range and do the same in a bedroom. We were both at turning points in our life, disillusioned at how time was slipping by so quickly. Christine was approaching thirty, divorcing, and she wanted to travel and use her languages. She felt that she had spent enough time working in organisations and was now interested in going to university. This was one of a number of relationships I had with women whose lives were at a crossroads.

Christine was also undergoing tests with a gynaecologist. The tests showed that she was probably infertile. I hope I was sympathetic to her, but part of me was relieved. Take away the fear of pregnancy and sex didn't have to be so traumatic, so angst-ridden, so consequential.

We both moved on from Nottingham. She got a job that involved a lot of travel, and then went to university as a mature student. I returned to Canada to submit my thesis and complete my MSc degree. The company offered to keep my job open but I wanted a clean break.

Christine and I wrote to each other regularly and saw each other occasionally over the next year. At one point we travelled together across France. I settled back in Britain around the time that my biological son approached his tenth birthday.

Six years later I was lying in bed with Maria one Saturday morning. The sun was shining through her bedroom window, we were naked and sated, and Lionel Richie's 'Hello' was on the turntable. Her long blonde hair decorated the pillow and she looked beautiful with the top sheet cast aside. Maria had the sort of body that made me take up drawing and photography. She was in her mid-thirties and had never had a child.

'I don't understand it,' she told me. 'You're everything I've ever wanted in a man.'

She paused and snuggled closer to me. We'd been sleeping together for several months. I had met her while she was working in a local shop. I would go the shop three times a day and she would fumble the change. After three months we realised the effect we were having on each other.

Maria had proved to be a sensual, huggy person who preferred to live an earthy life rather than an intellectual one. If our conversation was likely to become difficult she would say 'Let's not go there tonight' and that was good for me because I had a habit of overdoing analysis.

'You're everything I've ever wanted in a man,' Maria repeated. 'You're kind and considerate and good in bed. You're entertaining and good-looking and good company. You understand my moods. You've everything I've ever looked for, but if Laurence wanted me back I would go back to him.'

Maria had gone out with her teenage sweetheart, Laurence, for twelve years but they had broken up a few years since. After that Maria had discovered just how attractive she was to men, but recently she and Laurence had started talking to each other again.

Maybe another man would have fought harder to keep Maria. Maybe another man might have deliberately got her pregnant. I was neither of those men. The adoption had taught me how to let go of something important. I'd learned how to set people free in relationships rather than tie them into my life. I allowed them to experiment in the manner of a counsellor or nonjudgmental interviewer rather than as a boyfriend. I'd lost count of people who said they could be honest with me. Maybe she was trying to make me jealous so that I would react and promise her a future, but I took her more literally. I wasn't the sort of man who went round to a woman's house and beat on the door threatening harm, even though I was feeling the hurt.

Maria thanked me for being so understanding. I thanked her for giving me more sexual confidence and allowing me to jettison some fear and guilt in a physical relationship. Maria hooked up with Laurence again and got pregnant immediately.

'It was like he owed me a baby for what we'd been through

together,' she told me later.

Three years later, in the wake of my break-up with Valerie, I needed the right support and space to explore my feelings, and I was very fortunate that it came along. Through a friend of a friend I met an American teacher who was spending summers in Oxford for her Master's degree. Karen was undergoing change in her life. Her twenty-year marriage had hit a difficult point and she was negotiating details of a separation (such as who would move out and who would get the steak knives). Women at a crossroads were familiar to me. So were women at a distance. Long-distance relationships contained frequent intense moments that preluded lengthy separation. Partings at airports, train stations and alongside parked cars symbolised my greater loss.

Most of my relationship with Karen was conducted through letters and occasional phone calls, but she was soon an essential part of my life and our letters were lifelines. She was a major support for a book I was writing about my father's life, and she became a person I could talk to about most things. Karen and I made decisions in similar ways, enjoyed words and had the same sense of humour. We were both only children. After relationships loaded with hassle and torment I realised that a relationship could be enjoyable and safe. Also, Karen was older than me and didn't want children.

We became very close in understanding but distant in geography. I spent some time with Karen in the United States and she spent time in Oxford with me. Through Karen I again saw Oxford as 'the city of dreaming spires' rather than 'the city of screaming tyres' (as a probation officer had dubbed it during the joyriding heyday) or 'the city of dreaming cranes'. Karen helped me to enjoy Oxford through fresh eyes. I marveled once more at the delights of Radcliffe Square, the Holywell Music Rooms and Portmeadow.

My love affair with Karen continued until one summer when she needed more time to deal with her marriage. Here was another time when I could have fought harder but I was willing to let go. Had I fought harder, though, we would perhaps never have transformed our feelings into a lifelong friendship. I was far better than most men at making the transition from lover to friend. From my angle I didn't feel I had the right to make decisions and tell women what to do. I was still hearing a familiar subconscious voice: 'Nobody will take me because I made a mess of my life and got a young girl pregnant.'

25

Spring 2000

I phoned Louise Archer one evening after I'd spoken to Carol.

'We're both ready,' I said. 'Let's roll.'

'I'll send the letter to the name at the top of the list tomorrow,' she said.

'I'll be away in London the next few days but I'll phone my number to check my messages.'

'Be patient. This might take a while.'

'Of course.'

Two days later, while still in London, I phoned my home answerphone and discovered messages from Carol and Louise.

I phoned Carol first.

'He's been found,' she told me.

'Wow,' I said.

'He got the letter this morning and then phoned Louise.'

'Great.'

'Yes. He talked to Louise for half an hour. He's going away to think about it. His partner is expecting a child.'

'That sounds really good news.'

'He sounds all right. That's the most important thing.'

'As long as he's happy.'

'He said he'd had a good adoption,' Carol said. 'Do you know what day it is tomorrow?'

'Sunday.'

'Yes, it's Sunday. It's also Mother's Day.'

'He was phoning from his parents' house,' Louise told me. 'He got the letter and then went to their house, had a look at the records of his adoption and talked to them about it. Then he phoned me.'

'How did he react?'

'He was a little taken aback.'

'I'm not surprised. It must have been a shock for him.'

'Not so much shock. More taken aback by both birth parents searching for him.'

'He's in the instigating position from here.'

'Yes, he just needed time to think about it. He and his partner are expecting.'

'That's a lot for him to deal with at once.'

'He didn't see it as something he couldn't manage. He had the attitude that it was just part of life. He said he'd think about it. I think it will be difficult for him to say no to you.'

'Let's hope so. What's he like?'

'He was confident. It was like talking to a younger version of you. I had to stop myself from pulling his leg. There were little gaps in our conversation, like there are with you, when you're thinking about something. It was uncanny.'

'Did he talk about his life?'

'Yes. A little. But you have to remember that I had to do some validation at first. I had to make sure that he knew that he was adopted and I had to make sure I'd got the right person.'

'How did you do that?'

'Well, first of all I asked if he knew what this might be about. And he said that he knew he was adopted. Then I checked that I had the right person. I asked him the name of his parents' house. And he confirmed that.'

'Is it all right for you to tell me this or were you speaking in confidence to him?'

'At the end I asked him if he minded me passing on any of this information to his birth parents. He said that it was fine to tell you.

He said he had good parents and it had been a happy adoption. He went to university.'

Yes, I thought so. That would have been around the time that I was working in a Student Services department. I wondered where he'd gone.

'It's a lot for him to absorb,' Louise continued. 'If he decides to go forward this is about taking on two people – the birth mother and the birth father. I feel quite positive about it. He might come back after weighing it up and say we'll leave it for a few months.'

'But he's happy?' I asked. I felt like a parent.

As long as he's happy, that's the main thing.

'He said he was very happy. He's had a wonderful life.'

'That's the most important thing,' I said. I was really thrilled. My body was buzzing.

'There's a lot of things going on for him. He's being pulled in different directions.'

'He hadn't tried to initiate any contact with us?'

'No. He'd known that he was adopted but he'd never been very interested in looking. A lot of men say that. It's a question of building foundations. It's important not to go overboard. It's a slow process. Drip, drip, drip. He may worry about the impact of it all.'

'Of course. Well done. You've done a great job.'

Louise had been a superb intermediary. I think every family should have one.

I had planned another trip to the United States and decided not to put my life on hold. I had a writing project that I could take away with me. I was offered a base in New Jersey by my good friend Karen, who had come into my life twenty years earlier, shortly after my volatile relationship with Valerie.

My visit to the USA proved to be another surreal trip. On my third day at Karen's, her house and garage were struck by lightning and various appliances wiped out. The following morning, as we were looking at the damage to the automatic garage door, the mechanism suddenly sprung into life and trapped my fingers inside. I lost the top part of my right index finger. I was fortunate that the two doctors on duty managed to save my finger and stitch it back on.

'Will I be able to play the piano after this, Doctor?' I asked.

'Oh, yes.'

'That's wonderful because I couldn't play beforehand.'

I had always prided myself on my ambidexterity. Now I wrote left-handed, slowly and thoughtfully, until I upset one of my friends with the postcard I sent her – she'd thought at first that it was a ransom note.

Talking to Karen one day I suddenly realised that she must have been living near New York City at the time of the Woodstock Festival. She would have been in her mid-twenties then.

'Did you go to Woodstock?' I asked her.

'My sleeping bag went to Woodstock,' she told me.

'Your sleeping bag went to Woodstock?'

'My sleeping bag went to Woodstock.'

'You lent your sleeping bag to someone who went to Woodstock?'

'I did.'

'That would make a great title for a book on vicarious living,' I said.

'You and I could write that book from our personal experiences.'

'Or lack of them.'

My Sleeping Bag Went to Woodstock

I wrote it down on my list of books I might or might not ever write.

Three weeks into my trip Louise phoned to leave a message. I phoned her back from Karen's house.

'He says he's happy to receive a letter from his birth mother,' Louise told me. 'And he's given me his email address to pass on to you.'

I was doubly thrilled.

'Can he handle everything given a new baby in the family?' I asked.

'He says that if it gets a bit much he'll slow things down.'

'That is real progress. Thank you, thank you, thank you.'

'His adoptive mother is happy with contact because she was adopted and has had contact with her birth mother, but his adoptive father has some reservations.'

'Well, we don't intend to push in on the family or anything like that.'

I exchanged emails with my son. I sent him a short email introducing myself and he replied at more length. We were two adults writing to each other, comfortable, familiar, confident, excited. For me it was very easy from the start.

I have to say I hadn't had the desire to get in touch for thirty-one years but for the last seven weeks have found myself drawn to the idea, he wrote at the outset.

He had no regrets about his adoption and no feelings of blame. He sounded far better adjusted about it than I was, and I was immensely glad of that. In this early exchange I could feel guilt falling away from me like a badly tied bath towel around the naked body of a walking man.

I expect the choice you had was very difficult, he wrote. He wasn't in a rush to ask me any questions about the decisions over thirty-one years ago. But he would like to meet me.

And then, with his next email, there came a photograph…

While I was in the United States I was using Karen's email address. I wasn't yet a convert to the internet, I didn't have my own email account, but the photograph of my son's family was to give me a different perspective on new technologies.

I travelled to Boston, Massachusetts, to see my friends Graham and Joyce. It was three years since I'd read an internet magazine over someone's shoulder on the same trip and had decided that a search for my son was imperative. At that time Graham and Joyce had played a role in sparking my search. Now, three years later, they were there for another crucial stage.

Karen phoned me one weekday morning while I was in Boston.

'You have another email from your son,' she said. Then she hesitated before adding, audibly moved, 'And I think there's a picture.'

I asked Karen to tell me everything. We had no secrets from each other.

Karen read the email to me over the telephone.

'Some of his puns are just like yours,' she said, when she had reached the end.

'Do you think puns are genetically determined or as a result of socialisation?' I asked. 'Do any rhetorical questions ever deserve an answer?'

'I'm not saying anything,' Karen said. 'Shall I print out the picture?'

'Please, just to check that it is OK.'

I could sense the picture coming out of Karen's printer, coming out slowly, oh so slowly. I imagined it coming out upside down, face up, an inch at a time, spluttering occasionally, stopping and starting, head first...like a baby coming out of a womb.

'Oh my God,' Karen said. 'These are beautiful people. I am so happy for you.'

I was speechless.

'This looks like a really together family,' she told me. 'This is a young man who has apparently had a good life. It knocks my socks off. It's an incredibly beautiful picture.'

'Thanks, Karen. Thank you.'

'How am I going to get this to you?' Karen asked. She was only a little ahead of me when it came to technology.

Graham was at work so I talked to Joyce. We devised a plan whereby Karen would forward the email and photograph to Graham's work address.

'I'm just looking at this picture,' Karen said. 'You can recognise yourself in places.'

'Really?'

'I can see your mom in his daughter.'

'It sounds as though he's OK,' I said. 'It's wonderful.'

Whatever had happened in the adoption system, however much difficulty it had brought me, there was still him. He was real and he was healthy. It was all worthwhile.

I fidgeted around the house, waiting for the photograph...waiting for Graham, my virtual midwife, to come home from work.

During the afternoon Graham phoned me from his job at a start-up internet company.

'I've got the email from Karen,' he told me, in his usual calm, quiet voice. 'I've downloaded the colour photograph and I've made a black-and-white copy as well. And I think you'll be very pleased with them.'

My wait for the photograph continued. The next few hours seemed to last several days. I was an expectant father pacing up and down outside the maternity ward. I was a schoolboy staring out of the classroom window and willing the bell to ring. I was a hospital patient waiting for the doctor's bedside visit.

Eventually Graham walked through the door and greeted his wife and children. He took some papers from his bag and walked towards me. This was one of the best things anyone has ever done for me and I couldn't have imagined a better person to do it than Graham. He and I had been university contemporaries, but we hadn't really got to know each other until our paths had coincided in Cambridge a few years later. Now, twenty years on, Graham handed me the papers without speaking.

I sat down on the settee and looked at the picture. Here was my son's nuclear family and I was overwhelmed with delight. He was staring away to his left, past the photographer's right side, looking very content, wearing an open-neck shirt with the sleeves rolled up. His smile was gentle and warm, and I instantly trusted him. I saw something in his face that had been absent from my life since my father's death.

He was wearing spectacles and their rims hid the colour of his eyes. But his nose looked familiar and so did his forehead. The nose didn't look straight, or was that a trick of the camera? Could you inherit a broken nose, I wondered? My father had had his nose broken five times during his football career and mine had been broken once by a goalkeeper's fist. But that was after my son had been born...so how could that work?

He had a two- or three-day growth of beard, and I thought the designer stubble suited him. Maybe he was a reluctant shaver like me. The hair on his head was short and brown, and his eyebrows looked dark. I thought of Carol's father.

His ears looked normal enough. There was nothing to suggest that the six-week report on his 'odd ears' was correct.

I looked more closely at his partner, the mother of his children, and I thought she looked incredible. Her bright blue eyes stared straight at the camera. Her smile was radiant. She seemed determined, capable and beautiful. Her daughter had the same blue eyes. I knew immediately that he had chosen well. I had no real need to worry any more.

Graham and Joyce joined me and we looked at the picture together. My state of nervousness gave way to a quiet euphoria. I realised how important it had been to see what my child looked like. Here was a very familiar stranger.

During the next three weeks, as I travelled around the United States, various friends of mine stared hard at the photograph. They blew up sections of the picture, covered up parts of faces, compared my birth son's ears, nose and throat with mine, got out photographs of my father and put them alongside the picture, and altogether read far more into it than I could have imagined. But then, I suppose, I wasn't in a position to compare myself with the people in the picture.

'I'm envious of you,' said one close male friend who'd had no children of his own.

'Please don't be,' I said. 'This has caused me so much angst over the years and I wouldn't wish that on you.'

We laughed together.

In San Diego airport I made slow progress towards my plane for San Francisco. I was reading a notice alongside the scanner – DON'T EVEN JOKE ABOUT GUNS – when a female passenger checked me out.

'Aren't you that actor in *The Full Monty?*' she asked. I was considering whether to spell my autograph CARLISLE or CARLYLE when she added, 'You know, the old one.'

After we'd made our way through the scanner (without joking about anything) I stopped and talked to the woman and her husband.

'We loved that film,' the woman said.

I spent a few minutes recommending other films in the Yorkshire genre, such as *Brassed Off* and *Little Voice*. Then we chatted about a few other things and had a good laugh (well away from the scanner).

As they left to catch their plane, the husband turned to me.

'If you see my wife staring at you for a long time you'll know she's thinking of you at the end of that film,' he told me, showing a wry smile. 'And you'll also know how women feel when it happens to them all through their life!'

I had been mistaken for the actor Tom Wilkinson. It would happen a lot more over the next few years. Maybe it was because we were almost the same age, the same height (6ft 1in) and had both lived in Yorkshire during our childhood. Or maybe we were related. I wasn't sure who my relations were any more.

I emailed my son to thank him for such a wonderful photograph. It meant a lot to me and I'm sure it meant a lot to Carol. I sent him a photograph of myself, taken very recently in Oregon.

A week later, in Philadelphia, I met Ruby and her husband. We talked a little about adoption. Ruby knew some more about her biological father and I knew more about my birth son. Ruby and I had known each other for nearly twenty-four years.

My son was clearly happy with his life but he also recognised that he was part of the rat race. He was intrigued by my life on the edge but I was very impressed with his integrated life. He had lived the life that I might have led had I accepted the job with Royal Insurance on leaving school.

I had found my place on the edge of culture, an independent freelance person living a parody of the heroic loner. I was in the tradition of the cowboy who rides into town for one movie and rides out again. I was the private detective character in a book by Hammett, Chandler or Macdonald, the man who works alone and has brief liaisons with unsuitable women. But I was beginning to choose my heroes from the well connected, incorporated men who had followed careers, provided for their families and retained their integrity. My birth son quickly became one of my heroes. He had lived the life I wasn't able to. He was my book on vicarious living – *My Sleeping Bag Went to Woodstock*.

26

Nature or nurture?

I studied hard during my first year at university. Anxious that I wouldn't be bright enough, I compensated by being more assiduous than other students. I'd left a three-bedroom house for a student room with a single bed, washbasin and desk, but I saw more of the world in that student room than I had in my previous life. Through books I lived with the Nuer and the Hutterites and visited the 1930s' world of Keynesian economics. I experienced parenthood vicariously through Willmott and Young's *Family and Kinship in East London* and the Newsoms' *Patterns of Infant Care in Urban Community*.

Around about the time that my son was five I had a long chat with a psychology student about the importance of the first five years in a child's life. My fellow student talked about how John Bowlby and his colleagues had written extensively about attachment theory and separation anxiety, and the importance of the mother figure. I read Piaget and Freud for my Social Psychology course and wrote an essay entitled 'Why are the earliest years of a child's life thought to be so critical for the socialisation of conduct?'

I'd arrived at university as a statistician but started to think of myself more and more as a sociologist. With no knowledge about my own child I became interested in all children in some distant sociological way. When studying the nature–nurture hypothesis I came down heavily in favour of nurture. I became a firm believer in socialisation as the predominant force and locked myself into an ultra-sociological theory of socialisation. Nothing was genetic or hereditary to me now. I simply had to believe in adoption. A boy became a particular kind of man because of his upbringing. I sided with the social philosopher George Herbert Mead, who viewed minds as products of society.

I was also intrigued by the Reverend Thomas Malthus. In his *Essay on the Principle of Population* Malthus stated the case for population control. He argued that it was sensible to restrict population growth by promoting late marriage and moral restraint. Otherwise, according to Malthus, the population would grow to such a level that it had to be reduced to a manageable size by unwanted hazards such as war, famine, disease and pestilence. Neo-Malthusians of the 1830s argued that moral restraint was not possible so it was better to control population growth by contraception instead. This fitted in with other things I was reading at the time. I was convinced by theories of 'limits to growth' and 'ecological dangers'. I felt that the world needed saving. I was everybody's parent rather than my son's.

In my final year at university I did a course in demography. I studied population trends, birth rates, death rates and infant-mortality rates. During one vacation I signed the Official Secrets Act and worked in London at the Office of Population Censuses and Surveys. I came across Raymond Illsley's *The Sociological Study of Reproduction* and did an epidemiological project on Down's Syndrome. I looked at some of the bleaker sides of childbirth and saw the additional risks facing older mothers and fathers. (I already knew some of the problems of very young parents.) In my notebook I listed one question that puzzled me: *How come it takes years of training to become a doctor or an architect but you can become a parent or a car-driver with virtually no training at all?*

When I turned fifty I still belonged to the nurture side of the nature–nurture continuum. But I was becoming aware of some of the convincing research into genetic conditions. What I needed was some kind of experiential evidence. Eventually it came along, when I met my son and, later, his nuclear family.

27

Summer 2000

When I was back in England I had two months to pass before going to West Wales for a part-time job. I decided to spend those months in the Peak District, shuttling ten miles back and forth between the homes of two friends who were away a lot. I had a floating lifestyle with no house of my own, furniture in store, no car, no regular job, back in the mode of a teenager. Maybe I had never left my teenage days.

During this period my son and I talked on the phone for the first time and arranged a meeting. Our accents weren't that far apart and our sense of humour was compatible. He sounded personable and obliging.

'I'm happy to drive through to you,' he said. 'I do this all the time.'

I gave him directions to my friend's flat. I felt a strange sense of excitement and calm. As the day edged closer, though, I was reminded of meeting Ruby at Heathrow Airport fifteen years after our Kentuckiana summer.

Would I recognise him?

Would we have enough in common?

Would I be able to disguise how nervous I felt?

We had planned to meet on a Sunday. Normally I disliked Sundays because of the day's family associations, but this time I was looking forward to it. He phoned during his journey to say that the traffic was bad and he was running late.

'No problem,' I said.

What's half an hour after thirty-two years?

By this time I had all the physical signs of being lovestruck. Palpitations and butterflies in the stomach. Hands clammy with perspiration. Changing sleeping patterns. Relevant dreams. Anxious thoughts.

What should I wear when I meet my son for the first time? Do I dress up or do I dress down?

What should I work on while waiting for him to arrive? Should I choose something that gets me hooked in so that the time passes quickly? Should I find some mundane work that I can put down easily?

In fact I wore what I usually wear (jeans and a shirt), and the work decision was easy because I couldn't settle to work on anything. I had enough to occupy my mind. Had I given him the directions to the flat correctly? Do I look out for him or do I wait for the buzzer to buzz? I could see the car park from the window. I could sense a car arriving through the quiet.

Over the years I must have imagined our first meeting a thousand times in my head. I'd considered possible chance meetings like the one with Colin North when I was a careers counsellor ('Well, fancy that, you must be my son'). I'd imagined him knocking on the door of my tumbledown writer's garret flat ('Yes, I thought you'd call in soon after your eighteenth birthday'). I had fantasised about receiving a letter via one of my publishers and responding by post ('I am so glad you read my latest book and put two and two together'). I'd imagined an orchestrated meeting with other people present ('Doesn't he look like you, Carol?').

Like so many important life events, however, it is no use imagining them because it is always different to what you have imagined.

I heard the buzzer and my body buzzed with it. This was like a first date. It *was* a first date.

I let him through the main door and met him on the stairs to the flat. We shook hands and I made him a drink. He made it easy for me because he was accustomed to going into the premises of strangers. We settled in quickly and talked for a couple of hours. It was like seeing someone at a party and you both sense you've met before.

Have you been to…

Were you at that other party…

Or was it on the train one day…

I know where it might have been…

Hmmm, you think, this person reminds me of someone.

People in the adoption system compare this to putting on an old pair of slippers.

Part of me was sad that my parents were not able to meet him but mostly I saw the whole thing as a bonus to my life. Just knowing that he was out there, a likeable person living a life, was really good to know. I knew I would keep a respectful distance from his extended family. I had to respect them because he'd had a good adoption. Who's to say Carol and I could have done any better? We certainly could have done much worse.

I gave him a few photographs of my family that I'd collated earlier. I'd found a handful of pictures of my mum and dad. I had a nice one of Carol too. I had two or three of me, one about the time he was born, a couple from later in life.

'You've filled out a bit since this one,' he said, looking at a photograph of me at forty, lean and healthy.

'The genes are good,' I told him. 'My parents lived until their mid-seventies and were generally in good health. Carol's parents are still alive.'

'I've always felt confident about that,' he said.

I ran through a few of the minor health problems in the family.

It was a comfortable meeting, one that I will always treasure. The time flew past like it does when catching up with friends you haven't seen for a while. Finally I had a sense of who he was. Through the afternoon I sneaked glances at him as he walked, talked and sat. Knowing his name and seeing his image in a photograph had identified him for me, but seeing him in the flesh confirmed his existence, brought him alive. He had stepped out of a film still and into my home. I could now see his movement, his posture, his gestures and his gait. Not only was he alive but my parents were reborn, my grandparents revived, my lineage defined.

After the meeting I didn't feel any need to write down my feelings or process the occasion in the way I had done so many other times along my journey. In the space of a few hours the birth event had been transformed from my greatest trauma to my greatest achievement. Now I wondered what all my fuss had been about. I entered a quiet, contented period. I felt exhilarated and fulfilled, and my hitherto omnipresent restlessness seemed to recede into the background.

I can't remember much of the detail. Only the warm, calm glow of unspoken love. After the meeting I smiled for a month. And, with my friends, I laughed in all the right and wrong places.

Over three years had passed since I'd signed my contract to search. I'd set myself a target, worked hard on it and achieved my aim. The dénouement was more satisfying than I could have anticipated, but there was a big price to pay. Five months after meeting my son for the first time my body completely collapsed. But more of that later.

I phoned Nan, my search buddy, and told her about meeting my son. Nan and I had fulfilled our pact to each other. We had stayed in touch at long distance and supported each other through our searches.

I heard a story about a Welsh couple who had lived in England just before World War II. The couple adopted a son. When the bombs fell on their English town they returned to Wales and their boy grew up in a Welsh-speaking hotbed. He became a Welsh Nationalist, married a fervent Welsh Nationalist, and had children who were Welsh speakers. Then, in his thirties he learned by accident that he had in fact been born in England. That brought chaos in the family. By now I was a strong advocate for open adoptions. People need to be sure of their identity. What if people married unknowingly into the same family?

Carol met our son too. She phoned me the next day.

'Well, you certainly found the right one,' she told me, laughing.

She described the meeting in detail and then we talked about adoptive parents in general.

'I'm trying to get my head around the age of his parents,' Carol said. 'They are so much older than us.'

'I think they had to prove they couldn't have children and that meant they were in their late-thirties or early-forties when they adopted.'

'His father is almost exactly the same age as mine.'

'Yes, it's weird, isn't it? You'd have thought that would have struck the adoption agencies as weird.'

'His mother is about six years younger than mine.'

'It must be difficult for adoptive parents,' I said. 'They must put together some sort of story about adoption. Then we come on the scene and we are not always as down and out as some people might imagine.'

'I'd just like to meet his parents and thank them for what they've done. His adoptive parents have obviously done a good job.'

Carol and I were both enormously relieved that he'd had a good adoption. I continued to be shocked when I read about unsuitable adoptive parents. There were examples of adoptive parents who were abusive or crazy. One birth mother had searched only to find that her birth daughter had lived in care since the age of seven because her adoptive parents hadn't been able to cope.

'I'd like to hear them tell the story of raising him,' I said. 'Show us some pictures of him growing up. Some little tales.'

'Well, he's all right. That's the main thing.'

I could tell that we were both smiling. It had been a long and untutored journey and I would have preferred a better map and a proper mentor during the years before I met Louise Archer, but there were some wonderful events along the way. And amongst my angst there was always my son. He was worth every moment of the trip.

'I was reading something recently and I came across the term sperm father,' I told Louise Archer. We were upstairs in her house, in the room where we had been for our earliest meetings.

'Is that not like a sperm donor?' asked Louise.

'I don't think so. I think it's just another term for people like me. I'm a birth father, biological father, original father, real father, blood father, genetic father, hereditary father, putative father, natural father, proper father and sperm father. I suppose I'm a semen father too.'

'Oh, God help us, no.'

'But I'm not any of those names now. I'm just Andy to him.'

'Well done. The alternative names are just other people's labels.'

'Out of all those names I'd put birth father low down on my list, although probably not as low as sperm father or semen father.'

'Do you still prefer biological father?'

'I do. It was how I'd thought of myself for over ten years – from meeting Ruby to seeing the NORCAP lady around his eighteenth birthday.'

'When you met Ruby you found out very quickly about your adoption connection. At what point in a new relationship did you used to confide that you'd had a child?'

'Usually fairly early on. When we were just setting out.' I thought about that for a while. 'I think I was saying to the woman that you are taking on something difficult here, be careful of me, I've got problems.'

'How did they react?'

'Some would tell an intimate story of their own.'

We looked at each other for a moment.

'Can I ask you a question?' I asked.

'Of course.'

'How did my search compare with others?'

'It took a lot longer.'

'Because of involving Carol?'

'Yes. That was unusual.'

'I'd like to stay in touch with you, Louise. Let me give you my new address.'

I was moving to Wales where I had a nine-month contract to teach part time at a university. My time in the Peak District had been all about following my search through to a resolution. I had sacrificed parts of my life to do the search and now I was ready to integrate myself again in a world of relationships, love, new work targets and immediacy. I was ready to move forward. I felt very lucky. I could understand that other people's thoughts of searching could be truncated quickly by the scale of the task or the presence of a suitable life routine.

'Have you thought about publishing your collection of writings as a book about being a birth father?' Louise asked me.

'I have thought about that. It's a very tricky one. On the one hand I feel that it's a writer's responsibility to bring a birth father's story to print, especially as this angle on adoption has been relatively ignored and yet affects so many millions. On the other hand I wouldn't want to cause undue distress to the people in the story. Even with the names changed and certain characters amalgamated it's a very sensitive subject for those involved.'

'Maybe it needs some time to go by,' said Louise.

'Yeah, ten years.'

'Maybe not that long. See how the relationship with your son develops. Take him along with the project when the time is right.'

'I have a working title for my birth-father book.'

'Is it *My Sleeping Bag went to Woodstock*?'

'No. I think that one needs the subtitle *How to Live Vicariously Without Envying Others*.'

'What's your title?'

'Cat's in the Cradle.'

Louise thought about that.

'Isn't there a children's game called cat's-cradle?' she said.

'I've forgotten about that.'

Louise looked on her bookshelves for a dictionary and started thumbing through.

'It's a game where you loop string around your fingers and then pass it from player to player,' Louise said. 'It starts as a simple pattern of entanglement and then gets more and more complicated as it changes hands.' She found the right place in her dictionary. 'That's interesting. There's a second meaning. It's an impenetrable set of intricate regulations or instructions.'

'That sounds like the adoption system.'

'But it is definitely cat's-cradle and not cat's in the cradle.'

'Cat's in the Cradle is different. It's a song that has particular meaning for me.'

'Tell me how you got the title for your book.'

'Working title,' I said, correcting her. 'I'll write down the story.'

28

Cat's in the cradle

Living in Canada, in my mid-twenties, I shared a house with four other students and learned a lot from them. While we waited for meals to cook we played bridge and listened to music. That house was where I first heard Sweet, Gordon Lightfoot, Neil Young, Bruce Cockburn and many other contemporary artists. Sometimes visitors would arrive with guitars. Cathy perched on a kitchen work surface and sang Loggins & Messina songs. Bob sat on the floor and went through his John Denver repertoire.

In that lounge I first heard a song by Harry Chapin called 'Cat's in the Cradle'. Like many of Chapin's songs it had a strong narrative. Written for his son Josh, it told the story of a father who never had time for his young boy, followed by the story of the son who grew into a man who never had time for his father. The boy had grown up just like Dad. The song convinced me that I wanted to spend more time with my parents. I wanted to hear their stories.

Over the next few years I started collecting my parents' life histories. I quickly decided to write a book covering seven years of my father's working life. A very resourceful friend joined my project and together we interviewed a hundred people to collect a more rounded tale of the period under study. The experience helped me to see my father differently. I grew to understand his life and love him all the more. Also, my writing career was under way.

I was sitting at the kitchen table one day in 1981, reading a newspaper, when I saw that Harry Chapin had died in a car crash at the age of thirty-eight. I was mortified. I played Chapin's 'Cat's in the Cradle' over and over again. Appearing on the album *Verities and Balderdash* the song became an anthem to me. I started buying Chapin's LPs. Time and time again I returned to 'Cat's in the Cradle'.

I wrote a second book about my father's life, looking at how his early life (before I was born) had affected my childhood. I could see how patterns had emerged, how I had picked up details of his life that I had never known about. I spent hours talking to my parents. I wrote my father's story, but kept my mother's story to myself. That book about my father started out as a book about his life and ended up a book about my relationship with him in my developing years.

In the United States, visiting Karen in the late-1980s, at a time when Bourgeois Tagg was a popular band, I wanted to learn more about Harry Chapin's career. Karen took me to a Chapin tribute where a collection of singers reprised Chapin songs and stories. I considered writing a biography of Chapin but someone was already working on one.

Early in 1993, in the weeks after my father's death, I cared for my mother while organising my father's funeral and memorial service. One day I was out driving my father's old Saab 900 when I remembered that the car had a radio. I switched it on and discovered Radio 2. I listened to one song and was about to switch off the music when something familiar filled the car. It was Harry Chapin's 'Cat's in the Cradle'. Except that it wasn't Chapin himself. It was a voice I didn't know.

When I'd first heard 'Cat's in the Cradle' I'd resolved to spend more time with my father and write about his life. Sixteen years later, immediately after my father's death, Ugly Kid Joe's cover version brought me a new message – it was now time to explore my other father–son relationship. I vowed to find out about my birth son and how the adoption had affected me.

29

The next decade
Autumn 2000 to Autumn 2010

I entered a new phase of my life – my years of knowing him. Having completed the search for my son and established contact, I then faced another lengthy vigil of a different kind.

It began with a severe pain in the middle of my back. I saw doctors, osteopaths and chiropractors, but the pain continued, day and night, week after week. I'd always tried to avoid painkillers but now I was prescribed swathes of different types. I tried voltarol, tylex, valium, solpadeine, ibuprofen and dihydrocodeine, and carefully logged each intake so that I could abide by instructions. But nothing contained the pain.

Unable to sleep, I tried to walk off the agony. I walked for hours, especially at night, and wore the label off a packet of frozen peas by holding it hard against my back for so long. But the pain continued. Eventually I phoned my friends Alan and Barbara in Oxford.

'May I come and stay with you for a few days while I see my old chiropractor about my back problem?' I asked them. 'He may be able to pick up something from my notes and I need a second opinion.'

It was probably a twelfth opinion by now.

'Of course,' my friends said.

The journey to Oxford by car and train was by far the worst of my life. I went to Alan and Barbara's for a few days and stayed five years. All my friends now ask to see my return train ticket before letting me in their homes.

On my fourth day in Oxford I lost control of my legs, bladder and bowels. I became an emergency hospital patient. Suddenly I was as dependent on others as a newborn baby.

For over thirty years I'd been possessed by the loss of a son. Then I'd found him, met him, and was ready to get on with my life. Instead my body collapsed.

For over thirty years I'd presented myself to others as a fiercely independent man. Now I was totally reliant on nurses and friends.

For over thirty years I'd kept control of my life, despite the burden of loss, doing my best to manage the problem through writing, talking and searching, but now I'd lost control. The second and third times I met my son I was lying in a hospital bed. I had a non-Hodgkins lymphoma on the spinal cord. I was paralysed below T10.

On his first hospital visit he came with Carol. The three of us were together for the first time. I was lying in a hospital bed and they sat at my bedside. One of the original reasons for my search was to show him that he came from healthy stock. But now I wasn't projecting a very good genetic image. I was catheterised, chronically constipated and had lost proprioception in the lower half of my body. If I closed my eyes I had absolutely no idea where my legs were. I couldn't turn over in bed without help.

The meeting between the three of us felt relaxed and enjoyable. I was also more comfortable now that I was being treated with dexamethasone and morphine, specialist drugs that were capable of reducing the pain of a tumour on the spine.

Carol brought me pictures of her family and I suddenly realised that I was related to lots of people that I didn't know. But that felt all right. In an adoption system everything can be connected or everything can be too far away.

I was so glad that Carol and I had worked through a lot of our past history. A lot of the tension had gone. As I lay in my hospital bed afterwards, wondering what might become of me, I was so pleased that I'd solved the major mystery of my life. A hospital bedside is no place to start resolving the past.

Carol wrote to me after that meeting: *He is such a lovely person. He is so thoughtful and easy to talk to. For saying that the journey was only the second time I'd met him I felt comfortable with him and the time travelling went really quickly.*

His second hospital visit came as more of a surprise to me. He had been in the Oxford area for a work meeting and just turned up. When he walked in I was waiting to be transferred from an orthopaedic hospital to the cancer ward of another hospital. My bag was packed, I was dressed for the first time in four weeks, and I was sitting on my bed, my useless legs swinging over the side, waiting for the transport to arrive.

The other patients teased me about becoming institutionalised as I had been in the same hospital bed for almost all of January.

'We'll come and see you in the hospital Christmas pantomime,' said one.

'Shall we order you some letter-headed notepaper from the hospital print-room?' asked another.

'The time to worry is when they expect you to contribute to leaving presents for staff,' said my son.

'I think I'm going to need an Ovaltine trolley at 8.30 every night after I get out,' I said.

I spent a year in a wheelchair. At times it was a fine line between tragedy and comedy. My friend Anne travelled out of her way to visit me and said, 'Now you're trapped in a wheelchair I've brought all my holiday snaps from six weeks in Australia to show you.' I told her I could have been a stand-up comedian if only I could stand up.

At Barbara and Alan's house I watched the London Marathon on television solely to see the wheelchair races. I identified with actors in wheelchair roles – James Stewart in *Rear Window*, Denzel Washington in *The Bone Collector* and Michael Weatherly in the

Dark Angel series. Watching *Lady Chatterley's Lover* I imagined myself as Sir Clifford Chatterley rather than gamekeeper Oliver Mellors.

Alan and Barbara called me 'The Man Who Came to Dinner' and bought me a copy of the Kaufman and Hart play with that title. The book stands prominently on my bookshelf today as a symbol of everything these friends did for me. Under Alan and Barbara's wing I started a slow journey from helpless patient to functioning lodger.

Recovery was like restarting my life from scratch. In hospital I was a baby whose nappies needed changing. At Alan and Barbara's house I progressed from a crawling baby to a toddler. Then physiotherapists helped me through nursery and infant school by letting me play with pulpit frames, wall bars, rollator frames, crutches and sticks. After a year in a wheelchair and a year with sticks, I was back on my own two feet, as normal as I never was.

Alan and Barbara also nicknamed me The Teenager. Apparently it was because I didn't do much, had lots of phone calls, needed lifts, got up late, ate a lot and watched a lot of television. Over the next few years my hosts wondered if I would ever leave home, and one of my friends asked if Alan and Barbara would formally adopt me. I now had a new place in the adoption system.

The teenager analogy continued. I lived out part of the adolescence that I had been denied the first time around. I had teenager-like crushes on young girls and was tongue-tied in company. Back on my feet my body felt awkward and clumsy. I spent a lot of time in my room. When I started going into town on my own I felt like a teenager breaking away from home. I wrote an article for the *British Medical Journal* on 'the teenager theory of recovery' and a psychiatrist replied to say that issues of identity, independence, relationships and careers were the key 'growing up pains' encountered by teenagers and what mattered most was being understood, supported and loved. As The Teenager I could identify with all that he wrote.

I sped through my new life and became an adult again, but

I found it hard working out what kind of adult I now was. Part of me was a twenty-year-old who wanted to leave home and be adventurous. Another part of me was a thirty-year-old who wanted to settle down and have children. At the other extreme I was an eighty-year-old man whose body had let him down and might relapse into death.

I tried to process the impact of my search and the illness.

Who am I now?

What does it all mean?

What do I mean by mean?

I'd known him for about two years when he married his long-term partner. He told me that they'd thought long and hard about inviting Carol and me to the wedding but had decided against it.

'I agree,' I said. 'A wedding is not the place to start building relationships. I would hate to do anything to cause stress to your parents on such an important day.'

Carol and I had not yet met the adoptive parents.

'It's not going to be a big affair,' he told me. 'There aren't that many relatives.'

'I shall think of you on the day.'

And I certainly did. To use adoption parlance, I suppose you could say that Carol and I now had a birth daughter-in-law.

'It's interesting that they're getting married now,' Louise told me, when we spoke on the phone. 'Do you think there's any connection?'

He'd been in my life for over three years when I spent a weekend at his house. I watched him play sport on the Saturday and met some of his team-mates afterwards. He took me to his house and I met his wife and children. That was an overwhelming experience. All except his wife had my genes.

'It's amazing,' his wife said, looking at us both. 'You've even got some of the same mannerisms.'

'Really?'

'Yes.' Then she turned to her husband and teased him. 'You've even got the same sense of humour, except that Andy's funny.'

I modified my views on the nature–nurture debate. I shifted from an ultra-sociological theory to one that integrated heredity and development.

My son's children didn't know that I was a family relative. They had four grandparents already and didn't need to know about two more just yet.

'How long have you two known each other?' his oldest child asked him.

'About three years,' he said.

'How come you haven't been to our house before?'

'We've met in other places,' he said.

'There's a big wide world out there,' I added.

My son looked at me and whispered, 'And one day she'll be running it.'

I liked everyone in his nuclear family. It was very special.

'It's important that he gets to know his birth father,' his wife told me as I prepared to leave.

I went away euphoric, overwhelmed and confused.

After that we met annually or biennially. He was a busy man with an active family. He lived quite close to his parents and was admirably loyal to them. He and I met for coffee while I was visiting his area and he called in for lunch when he had a job that brought him to my part of the country. At those meetings I caught up on family news. On the phone we quickly recognised each other's voices and slipped into an easy bantering conversation that could have gone on for ever but for our busy lives.

My experience of loss had prepared me well for his life as a thirty-something. My role in the adoption process had taught me to interfere as little as possible. I could distance myself from his daily life, accept that he had his own established world and recognise that his family priorities were his own nuclear family and his adoptive parents rather than his birth parents. Carol and I tried to keep a respectful distance.

In some ways I felt not unlike other parents whose children had turned thirty and were living some distance away from home. Some of my friends visited their grown-up children only once a year. Their offspring were getting on with their lives and that was how it should be. It was the same with my son. He was creating his own personal history and that was wonderful.

Some years passed before I looked more closely at why I'd got ill. Surely it had to be connected in some way to the demands of the search. Was it because my body could only cope with so much emotional effort?

In the five years before my paralysis I had moved house eight times and lived in six different counties. I'd rarely taken a day off work during that period and I'd lacked a sustained, nourishing relationship. It had also taken me some time to recover from several major bereavements in the mid-1990s.

I don't think it was a coincidence that I got ill when the searching period was over and I felt a little lost. My stressful mission had ended and the fall-out began. I was like the retired person who stops work, moves to their dream seaside home, loses a sense of direction and falls ill. I was like the teacher who overworks during the school year and collapses during the vacation. The search had driven me forward but it was at a cost. After I'd met my son I was happy to relax about my life and take more space. Meeting him was what I'd wanted all my adult life. I could die happy. I could let my body collapse.

My son came to see me a few days before his fortieth birthday. By this time I had known him for eight years. He had my new address and said he didn't need directions. Despite entering the postcode correctly and the name of the street, his GPS system sent him to a street of the same name four miles away. I thought this was a metaphor for the whole adoption system. I'd gone all around the houses looking for him and people kept sending me to the wrong place. Now a system was making it difficult for him to find me.

He told me the story of a woman who had followed her sat-nav instructions to the letter and ended up driving into a river.

'She was a footballer's wife,' he said. 'That made it all the funnier.'

I enjoyed laughing with him. We chatted for two hours and I asked a neighbour to take photographs of us together.

Over the years I admired him more and more for the life he'd constructed for himself. He had a lovely family and a job that integrated him into the world. I no longer needed to write a book called *The Disconnected Citizen*, partly because I now had some family connection and wasn't a total outsider to society, and partly because two Harvard Medical School professors had saved me the trouble. Their book was called *The Lonely American*.

Once or twice a year, around his birthday or Christmas, I had a long conversation with Carol.

'I'd like to meet his parents,' Carol said one time. 'Not to interfere, not to criticise, just to tell them that they have done a great job.'

'Yes, it would be nice to hear more about his upbringing,' I said.

'His adoptive parents have been good to him and we have to respect them.'

'The decision worked out well as far as these decisions go. It's given him a good chance.'

'He doesn't owe us anything,' Carol told me, and I found myself nodding. 'We don't want to disrupt his life. It's not that we are disinterested in his life. Let him make the moves now. He has told us that we shouldn't worry about him.'

Some things had changed for Carol and me. But not everything. After forty-odd years of underworld birth-parenting our loss was no less raw.

'He's not their son,' Carol said. 'He is our son. We signed the papers and we respect the adoptive parents but at the end of the day a son is someone you give birth to.'

Of course Carol and I are left with an element of sadness that we couldn't have been involved in more of his life. There is also a lingering sense of unfairness – we produced him but we couldn't have him.

I stayed in touch with Louise Archer through Christmas greetings and occasional telephone conversations. Then one day we met for the first time in ten years.

'Do you remember how we talked about all the alternative names to birth father?' I asked her.

'Of course,' Louise said. 'I'm not sure I can remember them all.'

'I've discovered four more names for myself.'

'What are they?'

'Well, Jeremy Harding calls his birth mother Mother Number One or Mother One and his adoptive mother Mother Number Two or Mother Two. So I'm Father Number One or Father One.'

'That's only two more names, unless you want me to call you Mother One or Mother Number One as well.'

'I know. This is the best bit. Harding goes by chronology – the birth mother was the first mother – but I've just read an account in another book where an adopted person goes by the chronology of her conscious life. She calls her adoptive mother Mother Number One and her birth mother Mother Number Two. In other words she knew her adoptive parents first so her biological parents were the second lot of parents.'

'So you are Father One and Father Two?' said Louise.

'Yes. I am Father One, Father Two, Father Number One and Father Number Two. Simple, isn't it?'

'Simple. I've also heard "first father" applied to birth fathers.'

'So I'm a first father and a second father too?'

'I suppose.'

'How many names do I have for myself? It must be over twenty now.'

'Our society still has no words for mothers and fathers who

surrender their child for adoption.'

'Adoption takes something simple and turns it into something so complicated that it needs sentences and paragraphs rather than words.'

'Is Harding's book worth reading?' Louise asked.

'Yes. Take my copy.' I reached in my bag and took out Jeremy Harding's *Mother Country*. 'He got me thinking more about a number of matters, especially how adoptive parents can construct tales about the adoption. Do they introduce their child as an adopted child? Do they refrain from using words like offspring and issue? Or do they perfect a fiction? Here, let me read this line of Harding's.' I searched for a line I'd marked and read it aloud: '*How does a pair of miniature horses pretend to the rest of the ménage that the gangly specimen in their corner is the straightforward outcome of a good day's rutting?*'

'I've got a story for you about that,' Louise said.

'Please tell me.'

'A birth mother told me this one. It concerned the time she met her daughter and her daughter's adoptive parents for lunch. During the meal she noticed that her daughter's ears were shaped exactly like her own. She pointed it out. The adoptive mother responded by putting her hand on her husband's arm and saying, "Yes, Jim's got ears like that too".'

'Who needs fiction when we've got families?' I said.

'Exactly,' said Louise.

'I found another name for myself when I read Jamila Gavin's *Coram Boy*. One of the characters in the book, Otis Gardiner, is an entrepreneurial go-between who handles foundlings and gets money for placing them in orphanages. I wondered if I could be called a foundling father.'

'I think foundlings are babies left in public places, aren't they?'

'Maybe. I just liked the term. I'd like to think of myself as a foundling father. One small typing mistake and I could be on the Mayflower sailing towards America in 1620.'

'Ho ho,' said Louise. 'So how's life been for you? I remember you listing the purposes of your search soon after we first met. One was to free yourself up and see what came into your life. Have you felt more freedom?'

'Not really. On the one hand it's freed me from the conscious practicalities of searching, and it's freed me from the uncertainty about who he is and where he might be. On the other hand you cannot jettison thirty-odd years of behaviour overnight. I'm still a person who has difficulty in relationships and connects with other people who've had difficult life experiences. I'm still someone who stays outside systems and distrusts authority. I'm still someone who cannot read an adoption story without thinking about the birth father.'

I looked at Louise and then continued.

'The search freed me so that I could see my son as one particular person rather than the possibility of any male of his age, but my core persona was well established by then,' I said. 'If I'd thought that meeting my son might automatically set me up for a healthy relationship with a woman then I was living in Fantasia. I went on to have the most difficult relationship of my life. I got embroiled in an exaggerated soap opera that would have been too ridiculous even for prime-time viewing. That relationship was not more of the same it was a lot more of the same. I've not solved all my problems by completing the search.'

'One thing I remember about you is that you were often involved in a triangle,' Louise said. 'There would be three of you and then one of the three was killed off and it was usually you.'

'Yes, you're right.'

'It's difficult for birth fathers. Being a man you are supposed to be strong and supportive but you've let down two people – the child and the mother. Men are supposed to look after their women.'

'I've had to reconcile with both the child and the mother. That's my immediate triangle, the one that lay broken for years.'

'There's some recent work that suggests that the birth father's triangle is very different to the birth mother's triangle and the adoptee's triangle. The main diagram in the birth mother's world is the dyad of her and her child, and the third point of her triangle is more likely to be her parents than the birth father. For the adoptees the main triangle is the adoptee, the adoptive parents and the birth mother.'

'Adoption is much more complicated than a set of triangles,' I said. 'It's a big amorphous mass of overlapping polygons. You can start with a family tree, but then you have to extend the diagram because adoption also involves so many people outside the family. I think each adoption is a big constellation of interconnections that crisscross in ways that are often too confusing for one person's eyes. People have to compartmentalise them to cope.'

'I can see why you crave a simple life,' said Louise.

I had to laugh.

'I can live with the complexities more easily now but I wish I'd had some counselling earlier in my life,' I said.

'Why didn't you have counselling?' Louise asked.

'I don't know. None was offered at the time of the adoption. I think Carol and I accepted that the matter must never be talked about. Having the baby was like signing the Official Secrets Act. How do you enter counselling when you are told that nobody must learn about the event?'

'Our society didn't have a counselling ethic in those days.'

'For years I was traumatised and yet oblivious to the trauma. I didn't take it seriously enough. Eventually I couldn't leave the issues unaddressed.'

'It seemed like you learned how to talk about it when you were at university?'

'Yes. Lesley was a big help to me in bringing it out in the open. At times I must have been worried that I might break down if I had counselling. I had a need that others couldn't fulfil. I needed to talk about it but I didn't know what *it* was. I remember when I was about thirty a friend suggested I should have six sessions with a counsellor to see if that could help, to see if I could find someone I wanted to work with.'

'Did you do that?'

'No. I knew my friend was right but I couldn't bring myself to do it. I think I saw myself as on the other side of the fence.'

'More as a counsellor than a client?'

'Yes. That's how I saw myself. Then I worked as a careers counsellor during my late thirties. I did a part-time course to train as a counsellor during that time.'

'Do you think it's more difficult to seek help if you're a man?' said Louise.

'Probably. Birth fathers have a double problem – they are ignored by the system and they have to overcome any masculine stoicism that they might have. I was too scared or too macho to reveal all. My father had never had counselling and he'd had to deal with far more than I had to. If he could manage his life without counselling then so should I. Even when a relationship broke down and I was suffering more than most I didn't see myself as someone to be counselled. And when I did my counselling training I had some doubts about counselling. I didn't like the way I was left with unresolved thoughts and feelings at the end of an evening. I thought that fifty-minute sessions set a false time limit. I prefer sessions to go on until they reach a sensible stopping point. I found I ended counselling sessions with leftovers that I had to face again at breakfast or during the middle of the night. I didn't like that feeling.'

'You solved a lot through conversations with friends?'

'Yes. Conversations with friends and writing about issues. Maybe I was also worried about spending money on counselling. Maybe I was concerned that I would need far more than six sessions. Maybe I thought I would totally disintegrate.'

'Which came first – not having money or not having counselling?'

'I can't answer that. I think it was a two-way thing. I didn't feel that I deserved to earn enough money. But I think I avoided counselling mainly because I didn't understand the scale of my loss.'

'It's all about loss, isn't it?'

'I lost all sorts of things with the adoption. I lost him, I lost my innocence, I lost parenthood, I lost Carol, I lost trust in authority, I lost how my life and career might have turned out but for the baby.'

'Yes,' Louise said.

We allowed ourselves some silence.

'Thanks for all you did for me, Louise,' I said. 'I couldn't have done it without you.'

Louise shrugged her shoulders.

'I always felt that you were always in control of your own feelings,' she said.

'I might have appeared in control. I lost all control when I got ill.'

'You gave things a lot of thought.'

'I tried to.'

'Searches depend on the people. Some can go slowly and methodically and some have to rush into things. Some you talk to and they take note. Others go off and do what they want. And some people don't want to face up to their loss at all. People deal with it in different ways. Some refuse to acknowledge it.'

'Are you still doing intermediary work?'

'No, I gave it up when the new Adoption Act came in. You have to register as an agency and the cost of registering would be more than my earnings. You have to be a trained counsellor with reunion experience.'

'You have all that.'

'Yes and no.'

'I liked the way we did it,' I told Louise. 'By instigating the search I gained some power and control. I had been totally powerless for years.'

'The system has changed.'

'I think writers and therapists share certain characteristics,' I said. 'We know that what we see is not the whole story. There are secrets to be hunted down. Writers and therapists search for those pieces that are not obvious. We suspect that there is more going on.

We try to delve deeper than mainstream society permits. We touch wounds and attempt to make them better. Usually people are not ready for the skin to be pulled back, but we know that's the best way to heal wounds.'

'Have you written a conclusion for your book?' asked Louise.

'Do you think I should?'

'I don't know.'

'I'll have a go.' I looked at her. 'How would you summarise the place of birth fathers from the 1960s and 1970s?'

Louise laughed.

'OK, you want me to write your conclusion,' she said. 'Give me a moment to think.'

'Of course.'

She took some time.

'Birth fathers were excluded from the birth,' she said at last. 'Birth fathers were not on the birth certificate. Birth fathers were often omitted from the adoption file. Birth fathers' views were not taken into account. I reckon that birth fathers are about thirty years behind birth mothers in gaining their voice in the adoption process.'

For most of my adult life the adoption issue was like an elusive stowaway on board an enormous ship. The adoption incident didn't set me apart from people – I was able to form good relationships with other humans – but it set me apart from conventional stereotypes. Of course, I may have had other attachment issues because my father's own adoption hovered over our family, because being a football manager's son made me different, because we moved three times during my schooldays, because my mother came from a difficult background, because I was an only child, or because my emotions had been relatively unnoticed by my parents (who had their own unresolved stuff). But I'm sure that the adoption changed me. The adoption came so early in my adult life that I hadn't yet assessed my adult needs. Without the adoption I'm convinced that I would have committed myself to a relationship and a mainstream job. Instead I never properly mated and I became a committed freelancer.

At the time of the birth I knew I was young enough to start afresh so I looked forward and built careers. I coped with some of my angry and guilty feelings through the physical activity of sport or I turned them inwards. Ultimately the incident cost me part of my stability. Ultimately I was always dealing with pain. Ultimately it confused my girlfriends. Sometimes I'd be in a room with a girlfriend and I would invite so many ghosts, skeletons and ancestors that the room felt crowded and the girlfriend felt like she was one guest too many.

The adoption triggered my career as a writer. I searched for a lifestyle where I could breathe and grieve. I had the discipline and drive to write routinely and tried to write about difficult issues. But my writerly life did not come naturally to me. I had failed English O level first time around and my background was mathematics and statistics.

My writerly life was partly the self-punishment that comes from being a birth father rather than a parent. I was being hard on myself. I knew from the start that writing wouldn't bring in much money and that I would be condemned to living in flats with uncertain ceilings. Some birth parents might have punished themselves by running marathons but I did it by picking a writing career and becoming a desk triathlete. Writing was a paradoxical choice for me, a little like the young man with a stutter who wanted a career in broadcasting. Each completed book was an instalment on the reparations I owed. I was lost and floating for many years while I was acquiring the skills and language to tell this tale.

I sense now that the people in charge of the adoption system in the 1960s were generally looking after their own kind. Money was changing hands. The church was aiding and abetting matters of dubious integrity and morality. People like me were offered no advice, no assistance, no comfort, no counselling, nothing except blame and shame and more of the same. The church diverted my life into places it would not ordinarily have gone. For much of my life I didn't know what to do with my parenthood. I didn't know how to fulfil the role I had been assigned. As a father without a baby, I was like a manager without staff, a referee with no whistle, a surgeon lacking a theatre, so I diverted my frustrated parenthood into jobs and relationships with women. My classic example of surrogate parenting was working as a careers counsellor during my son's university years. My son went to a university less than a hundred miles from my workplace and I knew people who worked there. I met them at meetings while my son was a student.

My journey has been unconventional, at times painful, troubled and difficult, but I wouldn't have wanted it any other way. It gave me a very unusual perspective on the world, led to superb friendships and provided a very rewarding life of a different kind. The birth proved to be one of the unhappiest things in my life and yet one of the most joyous. The search enabled me to turn fatherhood from a trauma into something I'm very proud of. I can even forgive the people who formed and ran the powerful adoption system at the time. I concede that they believed in what they were doing; it was simply that they chose strange ways to create the goodness they aimed for.

In retrospect I feel very fortunate that I was able to search for my son. It was only possible because a number of factors came together at a particular stage of my life. My parents had died. I was able to distance myself from a destructive relationship and clear space in my life for the demanding process of searching. I'd learned that it was possible to take an initiative, I'd heeded all the signs and synchronicities that told me to search, and I had no-one very close to me who would be affected by what the search unearthed. Most importantly I simply had to deal with my loss before it destroyed me.

I haven't totally come to terms with the loss but I've learned to live around it in a different way. I now know what happened in my life, I know the impact of it, I've been updated on the story, and I've accepted that the event will stay with me forever. I no longer have any reason to fantasise around the issue of uncertainty.

I have come out of my search convinced about the value of knowing family origins and understanding medical, psychological and physical histories. And I have a more balanced picture of the nature–nurture hypothesis. Grandparents are as important as parents are. All family histories, warts and all, should be logged by a writer or interviewer for future generations.

At times I think I may have put as much time into my relationship with my son as any other parent has with their offspring. My direct contact with him has been slight but my indirect contact with him has been vast. I have written books about my family, searched endlessly for him, changed my direction as part of the search, thought about him often and always remembered his birthday.

If you spend over thirty years starved of a person you dearly love, devoid of dialogue with him, lacking sight or sound of him, all that exists is thinking, writing and imagining. Writing has been my way of coping with many of life's challenges. My writing career has been driven by a desire to solve my birth-father mystery.

Author's Note

It was only while writing this book that I recognised a pattern in my life. At a subconscious level I had re-enacted the adoption scenario in some of my relationships with women. Three relationship break-ups, in particular, affected me deeply by reprising key features of my son's adoption. I have written loosely about one such re-enactment in this book (the tale of Ivan and Irene in Chapter 2) but I have chosen not to write about two others that occurred after I'd met my son.

I can speak only of what seems to make sense to me. Other birth fathers will have different patterns of vulnerability to mine, perhaps determined by the circumstances of the pregnancy and the birth. In my case, I have spotted some key features that were present in those three relationship break-ups *and* in my birth-father experience. I suspect that these connections led me towards an abnormally powerful grieving process in those three break-ups, whereas my other relationship losses were more recognisable.

These were the features that replicated my son's adoption:

- A girlfriend of mine became involved with a new partner and I was the one excluded from the triangle (thus mirroring the adoption situation where the mother and baby were together for the first time and I was excluded)
- The new lovers were at a distance of 150 to 300 miles from me (as were the birth mother and baby at the time of the baby's birth)
- Their tryst happened at a time that commemorated an important calendar date, such as Christmas, my birthday or Easter (the original calendar date being the baby's birthday)
- The tryst happened in a place of symbolic importance for me (e.g. somewhere I had lived or had experienced something significant)
- The backcloth to my girlfriend's affair and our relationship break-up involved a death or loss that symbolically represented

the adopted baby (such as Ivan's suicide)
- I learned about the tryst after the event (or at the very last moment when it was too late to stop it happening)
- And, I felt completely powerless.

During the first two of these three relationship break-ups I had a whole set of extreme grief reactions. But the last one was different. Within a few days I had a breakthrough. I sensed immediately that I was playing out the loss of the adoption rather than the loss of the girlfriend. I suddenly saw my pattern. My trauma had shifted from the subconscious to the conscious. I came out of the grief much more quickly. A sense of warm calm returned. I started writing down how the break-ups had replicated the adoption scenario. I compiled my list.

I know deep down that these three women loved me and did not wish me any harm. They just happened to trigger my weak points, and clearly I was colluding to make that happen. I needed to avoid the places that the trauma sent me to.

Those three relationship break-ups fulfilled my need to revisit the circumstances of the adoption until I eventually saw what the adoption had meant to me. For me, adoption was about being estranged from the other two people in the triangle, adoption was about being miles away from loved ones, adoption was about movement and migration, adoption was about symbolic places (such as conception scenes, birthplaces and hometowns of close family members), adoption was about close family being symbolically killed off or lost, adoption was about not knowing what was really happening until it was too late, adoption was about powerlessness … unless, years later, I took an initiative and discovered a little more.

January 2012

Acknowledgements

I couldn't have attempted this book without the pioneering work of Gary Clapton, the birth father of British birth-father literature. I noticed his article in *The Guardian* (9 August 2000), read his book, *Birth Fathers and Their Adoption Experiences* (Jessica Kingsley, 2002), and appreciated his advice during my writing process. Celia Witney's work on birth fathers (*Adoption & Fostering* journal, autumn 2004) also reassured me that there were patterns in birth father behaviour.

The seeds of my book came in 2007, when Giancarlo Gemin and Michèle Lazarus independently asked me to give talks about my birth-father experience. My thanks to them for getting me started. For the first time I had reason to give more structure to my thoughts and notes.

While writing this book I was continually haunted by one particular line in *Handbook to Adoption* (Sage, 2006). The authors, Rafael A Javier *et al*, state clearly that the birth-father voice has been largely ignored in adoption literature, conferences and advocacy efforts. That lacuna needed addressing.

I was particularly inspired by Lynn Lauber's 'A Love Diverted' when I came across Sara Holloway's *Family Wanted* anthology (Granta Books, 2005). From there I discovered one of my all-time favourite books – Lynn Lauber's *Listen to Me: Writing Life into Meaning* (WW Norton & Co, 2004). 'Memoir writing,' according to Lauber, 'is a healing and avenging force.'

I am grateful to a number of other writers for some of the material on birth mothers used in Chapter 16: Suzanne Arms, *Immaculate Deception* (Greenwood, 1984); David Howe, Phillida Sawbridge and Diana Hinings, *Half a Million Women* (Penguin, 1992); and Julia Feast, Michael Marwood, Sue Seabrook and Elizabeth Webb, *Preparing for Reunion* (The Children's Society, 1998).

I must thank countless others for helping me to survive and develop in the years since I became a birth father. The following deserve particular mention because they engaged with me in turning-point conversations, shared parts of their lives with me, facilitated my healing process, helped with the search, provided feedback on manuscript drafts or aided in the production of this book. I offer my lifelong gratitude to Ian Alister, Karen Annesen, Judith Argles, Emma Blackburn, Carolyn Buckeridge, Cynthia Caywood, Sarah Coldrick, Christine Collins, Lynne Cook, Charlotte Cordingley, Gill Creed, Lawrence D, Helen Davison, Paul Dewey, Chris Donaghue, Liz Eades, Julia Feast, Jo Francis, RoseMarie Gallagher, Jamila Gavin, Geraldine Gordon, Nan Gourlay, Jeremy Harding, John Harding, Alastair Hignell, Patti Howe, Ilene Hoyle, Alan Jenkins, Barbara Jenkins, Bill Jones, Diane Kaylor, Jeanette King, Annette Kobak, Joyce Landau, Graham Lawes, Karen Lawrence, Sarah LeFanu, Melinda M, Karen MacDowell, Penny Morgan, Julie Nye, Jill Peay, Annie Peppiatt, John Polhill, Cheryl Ram, Manny Ramos, Penny Rhodes, Arne Richards, Kim Richardson, Louise Robinson, Shaila Shah, Angela Shanly, Nikki Simpson, Jackie Smith, Denis Spensley, Sheila Spensley, Brenda Stones, Sue Taylor, Amanda Toland, Evelyn Ward, Sue Wilkinson, Peter Wood, and members of BAAF Publications Advisory Group.

Finally, most significantly, my love and gratitude go to 'Carol' and our son, without whom this story would not have been possible.